# Communion and Contemplation

*Reflections on Friendship, Ministry and Prayer*

— DOUGLAS DALES —

Sacristy Press

**Sacristy Press**
PO Box 612, Durham, DH1 9HT

www.sacristy.co.uk

First published in 2026 by Sacristy Press, Durham

Copyright © Douglas Dales 2026
The moral rights of the author have been asserted.

All rights reserved, no part of this publication may be reproduced or transmitted in any form or by any means, electronic, mechanical photocopying, documentary, film or in any other format without prior written permission of the publisher.

Bible extracts, unless otherwise stated, are from the *New Revised Standard Version Bible: Anglicized Edition*, copyright 1989, 1995, Division of Christian Education of the National Council of the Churches of Christ in the United States of America. Used by permission. All rights reserved.

Every reasonable effort has been made to trace the copyright holders of material reproduced in this book, but if any have been inadvertently overlooked the publisher would be glad to hear from them.

Sacristy Limited, registered in England
& Wales, number 7565667

**British Library Cataloguing-in-Publication Data**
A catalogue record for the book is
available from the British Library

ISBN 978-1-78959-417-1

*For our family and in loving memory of my parents*

*Quid autem habes quod non accepisti?*
*1 Corinthians 4:7*

# Contents

Introduction.................................1

Chapter 1. Cicely Saunders......................9
Chapter 2. Henry Chadwick.....................20
Chapter 3. Alfonso de Zulueta..................32
Chapter 4. Michael Ramsey.....................42
Chapter 5. Benedicta Ward.....................54
Chapter 6. Donald Allchin......................65
Chapter 7. Peter Walker........................76
Chapter 8. Mary Clare..........................87

Conclusion..................................98
Further reading.............................119
Who's Who..................................123
Saints......................................124

# Introduction

*Beginnings*

Christian spiritual life may be thought of as a working loom, comprising warp threads with interwoven wefts, each with a distinctive colour, the frame as the legacy of childhood and upbringing within the life of the Church. After nearly fifty years as an ordained priest in the Church of England, it seemed appropriate to reflect on the pattern that has emerged like woven material flowing from a loom in the midst of all the clamour and racket of life's weaving.

It is a fitting moment also to pay tribute to those who helped to create the frame, and to those who unwittingly provided its warping threads—eight outstanding Christian friends, who were so kind to me as a young ordinand and priest. Reflecting now on their memory, example and teaching, it is fascinating to discern how they inadvertently opened many subsequent doors to experience, thought and prayer.

The sense that there is a pattern and purpose to spiritual life and growth in prayer reflects the fact that a person's life is always in the hands of God, whose Holy Spirit leads us into all truth. Christianity is therefore a continual education for disciples of Jesus Christ and there is thus a purpose to all that happens; this is a great gift of Providence.

Christianity is essentially an organic communion of friendship, across the world, and also across history, inasmuch as friends, holy places and books communicate in various ways something of the reality of the Communion of Saints. This book is therefore a study of how this can be so, for places and books as well as people certainly have a part to play in enabling the saints to draw near and to become friends. It has been a privilege to be able to study closely and to write about several such saints, as well as to have been able to visit many holy places at home and abroad.

The Communion of Saints as professed in the Apostles' Creed means, primarily, participation in the sacraments of the Church, Baptism and the Eucharist, but also Confirmation, Marriage, and Ordination, along with the other healing sacraments of the Church. The relationship between ministry and marriage is particularly close. To be a Christian is therefore never a solitary experience, and no Christian prays alone. The opening prayer of the divine office, "O God, make speed to save us: O Lord, make haste to help us", immediately joins our prayer to that of the whole Church. Christians are seldom aware most of the time of the extent to which their life and spiritual experience, and their wellbeing, is being nurtured and supported by others, seen and unseen, within the communion of the saints.

At the heart of Christian prayer is the call to contemplation and intercession as active participation within the prayerful communion of the saints. This book portrays the unfolding meaning of contemplative intercession as a distinct vocation of prayer. It charts a veritable pilgrimage into the hidden life of prayer as the central theme of life and ministry. The last chapter distils various thoughts about this, which have been discerned during times of retreat in England and also on Mount Athos.

My parents laid the foundation of my spiritual life and sense of vocation by their own example and unfailing kindness: they made the sense of God's reality and friendship immediate, real and natural. I was privileged to grow up within a loving Christian home and to experience the warmth and sincerity of those with whom we worshipped each week. The Anglican church we attended when I was a teenager was evangelical in its ethos, still using the Book of Common Prayer and the Authorised Version of the Bible, which have been my constant companions ever since. Bible classes and youth groups were places of friendship, open enquiry and discussion. Music also played an important part in our upbringing, as my father's family was very musical, and so we learnt to play and sing from an early age: my late brother, Martin, became a very gifted organist, composer, teacher and choirmaster.

When I was a child my family worshipped for a time at Baptist churches, as my father's family had deep roots in that tradition: on his mother's side they were descended from an Independent family, the Barrows, that had stood their ground against the bishops in the reign of Elizabeth I; on his father's side, they were descended from Huguenot refugees from southern France, who settled in eastern Yorkshire at the end of the seventeenth century. For my parents, this Dissenting tradition in England was an important witness to freedom of thought and belief, and also to a keen and active social conscience. My father's wisdom and humour and his wide knowledge exerted a profound influence on my own thinking and attitude to life. He was a true, kind and generous friend in every way and also delightful company.

My mother had grown up virtually as an orphan and in considerable poverty before the war, and her education had been disrupted by evacuation. Her desire to become a nurse had been frustrated by the sad illness of her stepmother. She was a kind and very gifted person, but also the casualty of a damaged childhood and frustrated abilities, whose mental health steadily declined. She was a very good mother in every way, however, who made us fully aware of the realities of poverty and hardship as the lot of so many other children. Our holidays in the north of England were always marked by visits to industrial towns like Bradford, as well as to the famous and memorable places like York. As an employer in the City of London, my father set a firm and effective example of how to handle both people and money, and he never endured a strike as a result.

We grew up with some Jewish families whose parents had escaped Nazi Germany, but as children we were never aware of their background until the father of one of them, who was a doctor, died by suicide. I was about fifteen at the time and my parents explained that the shadow of the swastika still scarred and destroyed the lives of so many. We were brought up to take seriously the ravages of modern history, and to care about human rights and the persecution of Christians and others in lands under dictatorship. Racism and snobbery had no place in our home, and we were firmly reprimanded if we ever brought back chatter of this kind from school. They taught us about the evil of antisemitism so that we took it very seriously, and they insisted on the importance of toleration towards other religions that was based upon genuine interest and respect.

Both my parents had a lively sense of history and art and were well-read. There was no shortage of books in our home, although we never travelled abroad as a family. Instead, we got to know Kent with its rich history, and later other parts of England as well, like Cornwall, Norfolk and Yorkshire. The cathedrals at Canterbury and Winchester were great favourites, and we were often in London during school holidays, attending concerts, visiting museums and art galleries, as well as St Paul's Cathedral and Westminster Abbey. Central to this sense of history and tradition was the Bible, which my parents always treated with great respect and which we were encouraged to read each day. They would always answer our questions if they could, and they had no time for dogmatism, party or factionalism in Christianity. They also had many friends who were clergy in other denominations, and their outlook was robustly ecumenical. They supported the work of Keston College in monitoring human rights abuses in the Soviet Union and were active supporters of the missions of the Church at home and abroad.

They encouraged us to take seriously the nature of Christian vocation, however it might be expressed, and they supported my decision to become an Anglican ordinand and priest, even though they had a healthy scepticism towards the blandishments of the establishment and warned against the hazards of clericalism. My first degree at Christ Church, Oxford, was in Modern History, and this provided a sound basis for then studying Theology, as Christianity is best understood from a historical perspective. For a priest, theology should never become an academic end in itself, nor should it be divorced from the life of prayer.

The clergy whom I knew as a child and young person were all very good people; not always great preachers, but utterly sincere in their understanding of Christianity. Martin Preston, the chaplain of my school, St Dunstan's College in south London, to which my father had gone before me, left a lasting impression, and he set a fine example which provided the foundation of my own later ministry as Chaplain of Marlborough College. He introduced us to the questions that were besetting the Church of England in the 1960s, notably South Bank Theology associated with the then Bishop of Woolwich, John A. T. Robinson. He also kept us informed about the work of Vatican II, and also the struggle against apartheid in South Africa and the civil rights movement in America. Belief in Christianity was never compelled at school, but he and others certainly made its relevance and importance to modern society abundantly clear.

My parents welcomed the teenage children of a Protestant family in Austria, who made many visits to our home, and who have remained firm friends ever since. This experience was deeply enriching and informative, and Lower Austria with its monasteries and mountains and the beautiful Wachau valley of the Danube became a second home. I went first to Italy during the Easter holidays in 1968, to Florence and also to Rome, and this was my first encounter with the Roman Catholic Church. Between degree courses, I was able to travel in 1974 to Kenya and Tanzania as a guest of various CMS missionaries working there. Africa reaches deep into the soul and the memory of church life there helped to sustain my own vocation as an ordinand when the going got difficult. As a result of these memorable visits, I received an abiding sense of the global nature of Christianity.

No living people are mentioned in this book, however, as it seems invidious to have to choose among so many good friends; but three bishops whom I knew well as a student set fine examples and were very helpful in enabling me to discern my own vocation to become an Anglican priest. The first was Philip Goodrich, then vicar of Bromley, and later Bishop of Tonbridge, and then of Worcester. His enthusiasm for ministry and his cheerful and robust good sense were memorable and motivating; he and his wife proved true friends to my brother and myself as teenagers and for long afterwards. Neville Langford-Smith was the Bishop of Nakuru in Kenya, who welcomed me to his diocese and enabled me to travel with a missionary priest and friend across Tanzania to Burundi and back. He and his wife came from Australia, but they had taken Kenyan citizenship in order to support the life of the church in a newly independent country. Finally, Ronald Goodchild, the Bishop of Kensington, who was the bishop who ordained me as a deacon in 1977 and then as a priest in 1978. He and his wife also proved to be good friends to us and our family long after he retired from London to live in north Devon. He was the most effective bishop with whom I have ever worked and a model for anyone learning to serve as a priest.

Marriage and ministry are closely conjoined, both being bound by life vows, and we were blessed by being married by Archbishop Michael Ramsey in 1977. My beloved wife, Geraldine, and our children and grandchildren, are the greatest blessing in my life, for whom this book has been written with deep gratitude and affection.

1

# Cicely Saunders

*Cultivating empathy*

The person who most equipped me pastorally to be a priest was undoubtedly Dr Cicely Saunders. Through the encouragement of her principal colleague, Dr Mary Baines, a friend of my parents, she invited me in 1975 as an ordinand to participate in the training course being offered to doctors and nurses at St Christopher's Hospice in South London. This was in the newly developing field of care for those with terminal illnesses, which she had pioneered there. The following year, Dr Saunders invited me to return to the hospice to prepare the way for the appointment of a full-time chaplain. Dr Baines became a lifelong friend, and we exchanged a lively correspondence for many years, as palliative care became widespread throughout the UK and then across the world. As we often agreed, this has been one of the most benign contributions made by England to the needs of human beings everywhere, resulting in a true revolution in attitudes towards the care of the dying and the bereaved.

Cicely Saunders was a remarkable and memorable person, and I was privileged to secure her friendship and encouragement. Her Christian faith was radiant, as was her vision of what needed to be done. With great determination and vision, she trained first as a nurse during the war, then as a social worker, before becoming a doctor in 1957. Within ten years, and against the odds, she secured significant backing for her mission to address the plight of those dying of terminal illness, for whom no effective or systematic care was then available. I attended the opening of St Christopher's Hospice with my parents in 1967. This hospice pioneered the holistic care of those with terminal conditions, seeking to mitigate their chronic pain and other symptoms, while supporting their families during the last months of their relative's life. It also developed and provided active bereavement care of families after a patient's death. As a result, the hospice became the focus of a remarkable community of local support, as well as an active medical and nursing training centre. It was a tangible example of what could be, and would be, achieved elsewhere.

The foundation of St Christopher's Hospice and the development of a systematic programme of pain and symptom control sprang from Dr Saunders' own deep Christian conviction that scientific research and careful medical practice and pastoral care could result in overcoming the fear of dying for most patients and their families. Hers was also a determined and principled response to secular pressures for euthanasia, which were highly articulate, then as now. Euthanasia was nonetheless still viewed askance by many Jews, Christians and others in the light of what had recently happened in Nazi Germany. Dr Mary Baines was responsible for overseeing the ambitious training programme offered by the hospice to doctors and nurses from near and far, as well as developing the practice of widespread palliative care by GPs and others. The aim was to keep people at home for as long as possible. Hospice care spread throughout the UK and the English-speaking world until it became available in many of the poorest countries, as well as in the European countries emerging from Communism. St Christopher's Hospice embodied a fruitful collaboration between Christian belief and rigorous scientific and psychological research and practice, which among other things also transformed pastoral care of the bereaved. It represented a sound and creative partnership between state provision of healthcare and private charitable initiative.

Talking and working with Dr Saunders and her colleagues taught me the vital Christian principle of *empathy*, which means not just coming alongside those in need out of sympathy, but actually trying to understand them as whole people, by listening carefully and humbly to their story. Her principle was: "You matter because you are you; and you matter to the last moment of your life." She also taught awareness of what she called "total pain"—physical, emotional, social *and* spiritual. She believed in caring for people "for better, for worse … until death do us part". To work with her at the hospice was to be plunged directly into the demanding realities of suffering and listening, as well as all the practical nursing care of people's physical and other needs before and after death. It was a humbling and formative experience, which laid the foundation for all my pastoral ministry as a priest, in parishes and also in hospitals.

In parish ministry, a priest has to be all things to everyone in terms of accessibility and trust, and I was fortunate to be trained by two excellent incumbents in Shepperton and Ely. In the Church of England, a priest serves anyone in the community who may need help, whether they go to church or not; by living among them one should become someone respected and available. The kitchen table is often the second altar as a priest sits with a person or a family to listen to all that they have to say. It is, of course, a privilege to be made welcome in homes of every social background, and it is also a great education. While I was Chaplain of Marlborough College, we were able to restore links with the parish in London of St Mary's Tottenham, which was founded by the College at the end of the nineteenth century. This is a now a dynamic Anglo-Catholic and multi-racial Christian community, and it was a regular delight to be able to work with the clergy there during many years, both of whom remain firm friends.

How baptisms, marriages and funerals are conducted matters supremely, as the memory of them will last for years, as living experiences of Christian love and truth in action. The cure of souls is a great and lifetime's art that expresses and deepens the sense that every human person is of equal worth as a child of God. A priest is called to be an ambassador of Christ and also a fellow-worker with the Holy Spirit in the care of others, serving as a link in the chain of divine love and outreach. Empathy means sitting where the other person sits, genuinely feeling their pain, and supporting individuals and families round the difficult corners of life. It also means working closely with other caring professionals and supporting them in their demanding work in hospitals and in the community.

How can empathy be taught? Luke's Gospel portrays most vividly the deep empathy of Jesus, and it was my privilege to discuss this Gospel with hundreds of teenage pupils, boys and girls, as Chaplain of Marlborough College for 28 years. A priest teaching the Bible to the young is also their pastor, and even their friend in a way. A chaplain also has pastoral responsibility towards all who work in the school, as well as to the families of pupils, past and present. A chaplain has also to make sure that that those of other faiths or other Christian traditions receive the support and encouragement that they need for their spiritual development while at school. The key to effective teaching and pastoral care of the young is the willingness to encourage, hear and answer their endless questions. Once again, empathy is essential, as young people are sensitive and sometimes far from confident, and they always need to be affirmed in a kind and consistent manner. They can never be compelled to believe in Christianity, and fortunately chapel services were largely voluntary at Marlborough College, complemented on Sundays by an active programme of charitable and other social outreach. For in the wise words of T. S. Eliot: "A Christian education should seek to instil informed Christian categories of thought without ever trying to compel Christian belief."

Teaching Luke's Gospel to the young, in the classroom and also as part of Confirmation preparation, was an extraordinary experience. Young people have a keen sense of justice and also of compassion, and they warmed to the many stories of Jesus that addressed and embodied these. Their reaction to stories like the Good Samaritan, the Rich Man and the Beggar, the Prodigal Son, or the woman who washed the feet of Jesus was immediate and clear. For example, one of them observed, about the healing of the Paralysed Man, "that at the command of Jesus his sins got up and left him, and so he was able to get up himself!". The ethos of Luke's Gospel is also perfect for teaching wider human sympathy and compassion, a recognition that social justice matters, and that human rights, accountability and the rule of law are a vital concern for us all. It is not difficult to build bridges from this Gospel across to the ethical teaching of other religions, notably Judaism and

Islam, and empathy towards those of other faiths or of none is essential in modern society. Examples of those who stood for freedom and justice always appealed to the young and demonstrated the relevance of the gospel message: Nelson Mandela or Dietrich Bonhoeffer, or those still suffering under Communism.

My own approach to teaching Religious Education, as it was then called, was anchored in modern history, which I had studied at Oxford. Indeed, it was the memory and example of Dietrich Bonhoeffer in particular that had been an important influence in my own decision to become a priest. The minister of the church in Sydenham in South London to which my parents first went had known Bonhoeffer before the war as the pastor of the German church there. I kept in close touch with the work of Keston College, as it monitored the abuse of human rights and the suppression of religious freedom in Communist countries. My own visits to the Soviet Union as it was collapsing in and after 1989 enabled me to bring first-hand accounts of the impact of persecution to my pupils.

The study of history therefore is one of the best ways to cultivate intelligent compassion, understanding and empathy. I was very well taught at St Dunstan's College and then at Christ Church, Oxford, and the study of history has always been my first love. During those years at school and as an undergraduate, my interest was in modern history. I soon realized that it is vital to understand the history of our own country, its Christian values and its unique constitution. I also plunged into European history with the memory of the two World Wars in the background, and also the awareness of persecution continuing in totalitarian dictatorships around the world. The writings of Hannah Arendt provided a sure guide to the issues at stake. Only by studying both sides of a conflict can any real understanding be achieved: critical empathy of a particular kind is required, which should be well informed by open access to original sources as well as to foreign historiography.

Travel also enlarges empathy, and I have been fortunate to be able to visit many countries in Europe and beyond. To visit the battlefields and cemeteries of the two World Wars, or to visit the site of a concentration camp, is to be seared for ever. Why was there so much suffering, and so often by so many young people? Only by standing in the vast plains and forests of eastern Europe can the scale of wartime devastation be sensed, and it is impossible for a westerner to understand the depth of fear in Russia that has endured three terrible invasions in the twentieth century, and the loss of lives totalling the entire population of the United Kingdom. Antisemitism is another area of particular difficulty that stretches sympathy and empathy to the limit, not least in relation to the state of Israel and the plight of the Palestinians. Understanding of its long and complex history is indispensable for thinking about conflict in the Middle East today. The impact of Ottoman rule in Greece and elsewhere in south-eastern Europe is conveyed by the grim portrayals of martyrdom in the narthexes of many Orthodox churches. The study of history also precludes any romantic view of colonialism, where so much hurt was done in ways that still reverberate today.

The historian has a vital role to play in an open society by examining dispassionately the causes of political and social problems, issues, and conflicts. One of the great strengths of European culture is the high quality of historical research and writing. But one of the great lessons of foreign travel is that insecurity is a principal root of conflict, and that trauma and injury leave abiding wounds in the mentalities of so many countries. This reveals the limits of empathy inasmuch as someone from "the sceptred isle" of England can hardly enter into such an inheritance of pain, in societies where the past is not the past. But a Christian historian can listen carefully and respectfully; and by so doing affirm the value and dignity of witnesses.

Art too has an important part to play in enlarging empathy. I first went to Italy as a schoolboy, to Florence, Pisa, Lucca, Siena, and Rome itself for Easter in St Peter's Basilica in 1968, and I was struck then by the painting of Duccio in Siena in particular and of those around him at the turn of the thirteenth century. This was the century when the artistic vision of Europe was being transformed by the witness of St Francis of Assisi, a transformation that is evident in the art of Cimabue, Giotto, and Masaccio in the great basilica in Assisi and elsewhere. The humanity of Jesus and the reality of his suffering were seen anew and conveyed with great sympathy, pathos and beauty. It was the genius of Duccio to go one step further in terms of an empathy that enabled him and those around him to convey the way in which the divine glory of the transfigured Christ shines through the fragile reality of his humanity. The art of this period has always been central to my own appreciation and spiritual understanding, and this is just one example of the way in which visual art can transform sensibility and deepen empathy. Christian art in every generation has been able to achieve this because the root of all Christian art, Western and Eastern, springs from the Transfiguration of Christ, through whom the glory of God is expressed in a human person.

Music also stimulates a deeper understanding of human life and nurtures empathy. I was brought up in a family that valued music, and my uncle and my brother were both gifted church organists. I learnt to play the piano and the organ and was also a chorister at school. Music plays a comparable role to art by greatly deepening sensibility and empathy, often in a forceful and moving way. Two examples of Christian music spring to mind which have been central to my own spiritual life: the *St Matthew Passion* by Johann Sebastian Bach and the *Requiem* by Wolfgang Amadeus Mozart. I sang the *St Matthew Passion* at school and have always listened to it, if I can, every Good Friday ever since. I have also heard these great pieces of Christian music sung in various places abroad, which have transformed their meaning for me. For example, I recall hearing the Mozart *Requiem* being sung in one of the lovely Gothic churches in Riga in Latvia. My host said that only the suffering of Mozart at the end of his life could produce such music; and I replied to her that only a people who had suffered so much could sing it in the way they had just done. I heard the *Requiem* sung again in Prague on a visit there with our two sons, marking the anniversary of the Soviet invasion of that country in 1968.

Listening to many hours of Orthodox Byzantine chant in the services of monasteries on Mount Athos conveys not only its deep spirituality, but also a long history of suffering under persecution. It was the genius of Rachmaninov to transform such a rich inheritance in his church music that conveys something of the depths of Russian Orthodox Christianity. I remember hearing his setting to the Divine Liturgy being sung in the refectory church of the Monastery of St Sergius, north of Moscow, at Easter in 1991. Such music feeds and transforms the soul, and I consider that Christian art and music are decisive witnesses to the existence of God, as beauty is the most important sign of His reality. Christian art springs from belief in the Incarnation and derives its strength from that reality. Human beings respond to such beauty and also express it in art and music, because they share a profound creative affinity with God, being made in His image and likeness.

2

# Henry Chadwick

*The love of learning*

I first got to know Dr Henry Chadwick as Dean of Christ Church, Oxford, when I was President of the Junior Common Room there in 1972. Various contentious issues engaged us both, and out of these discussions a firm friendship was born, often sustained by long walks around Christ Church Meadows. Dr Chadwick had been Regius Professor of Divinity in Oxford before becoming Dean of Christ Church, and in 1979 he returned to Cambridge as Regius Professor of Divinity, before becoming Master of Peterhouse in 1987. He was the most distinguished Anglican scholar and theologian of his day, an engaging and memorable lecturer, and a kind but demanding mentor and teacher. Gracious and formidable in equal measure, his first challenge to me as a new undergraduate reading history was, "never build bricks without straw!". Every time I enter the Lower Reading Room in the Bodleian Library, I remember him and his firm advice. Dr Chadwick generously taught me the New Testament, Patristics, and Early Church History papers while I was reading Theology as a graduate in Christ Church and preparing for ordination in the Church of England. He also set a fine example as a priest in leading divine worship in the cathedral, where his love of music matched his deep sensibility towards the liturgy. My most abiding memory is of his unfailing kindness and generosity, which were always encouraging and stimulating.

Dr Chadwick imparted a keen sense of the importance of Church history, and of the scholarly vocation and work of Church historians as vital to the Church's unity and identity. He considered that a church that did not regard, value or understand its own past was like a person gradually losing their memory. Such wilful amnesia also precludes any ability to understand deeply the traditions of other Christians, or even other religious traditions. He brought his own unique range of knowledge to bear in supporting the Archbishop of Canterbury, Michael Ramsey, in the creation of ARCIC [The Anglican and Roman Catholic International Commission] in order to address and begin to resolve the historic differences between the Anglican and Roman Catholic Churches. Dr Chadwick demonstrated by his own writings the way in which the Christian past is actually a living past that influences the present, for good or ill. Empathy towards the manifold inheritance of Christianity must be rooted in accurate knowledge of the past in order to understand each side of an issue, and to discern the truth within each strand of Christian tradition. In practical terms, this requires extensive mastery of American and Continental scholarship and therefore of foreign languages. Dr Chadwick's scholarly reputation abroad was as formidable as it was in England.

He taught that the New Testament must always be approached as a unique piece of history, its language steeped in the Greek version of the Old Testament as well as in the teaching of Jesus. Speculative proliferation of hypotheses, however, too often obscures the direct force and integrity of the text. It is, of course, frustrating for historians that there is so little material remaining that directly impinges on the actual formation of the New Testament. Nonetheless, careful study of its precise historical context, particularly in the light of the Apostolic Fathers and of the Septuagint, is the key to understanding its message. Dr Chadwick's own sense of irony and detachment opened the door to the thought of St Paul in particular: he did not think that a saint should ever be put on a pedestal. Indeed, he once said, teasingly, that "a saint is someone whose life has never been fully studied and written up".

He himself did much to place the memory of St Peter and St Paul in Rome on a secure historical footing, by examining closely the traditions surrounding the places of their burial and commemoration. He also imparted a sympathetic understanding of the peculiar demands of the papal office by the way he spoke about St Leo the Great. He knew intimately the significance of Leo's *Tome*, which was sent to the Council of Chalcedon in 451, and he could chart his way surely through all the controversies of the fourth and fifth centuries in a way that alerted a person to the very precise issues and tensions that surrounded each of the various Church councils of that period. He was also a sure guide to the demanding theology of the Cappadocian Fathers. Dr Chadwick's approach to the way in which Eusebius composed his famous *Church History*, along with his encomium for the Emperor Constantine, was an education in the challenging art of reading such a text and discerning all that it was conveying, intentionally and unintentionally. His study of Boethius is another monument to his critical and sympathetic understanding of someone paying the price for his own commitment to truth in the midst of a complex political situation. Such a disciplined formation stood me in very good stead later when studying the *History of the English Church* written by the Venerable Bede.

Dr Chadwick made the study of Patristics hugely enjoyable, and his most abiding gift as a theologian was to introduce me to St Augustine with whom he had such a deep and natural sympathy. Augustine was a sensitive and introspective seeker after divine truth, and also a person with a keen musical and aesthetic sense. Dr Chadwick orientated his teaching far beyond the dictates of the looming examinations, proving a sure guide through the vast literature surrounding the person and thought of Augustine. As a result, as for many before me, Augustine became the father of theology, the fountainhead of a rich tradition of thought and insight into divine truth, and also into the psychology of human beings. In a way, Augustine's *Confessions* is the best accompaniment for anyone embarking on the vocation of becoming a Christian priest: the uncertainties surrounding Augustine's own quest for God; his grappling with the complex and elusive nature of reality itself; his gradual sense of the unique significance of Christ as the Mediator; and finally his submission to the humble discipline and frustrations of the Christian Church, with which he engaged to the end of his life as Bishop of Hippo in North Africa.

For any Church historian, Augustine's *City of God* is a most vital resource and inspiration. Writing at a time of widespread upheaval affecting the western Roman Empire, when Christians and pagans alike were alarmed at the shaking of familiar foundations, Augustine's prophetic vision and critical insight projected a vast panorama showing how divine providence is at work within all the turbulence of human history. The Church is the sign that this is so—that there is truly "the City of God", even though this is not to be narrowly identified with the visible structures and limitations of any one of the actual churches. For in the midst of all the apparent chaos, the divine voice declares, "Behold, I *am* making all things new."

For any priest and teacher of theology, Augustine's remarkable work *On the Trinity*, backed up by his profound commentaries on St John's Gospel and on the Psalms, provide an inexhaustible well of wisdom from which to draw. No less interesting are his various writings about the opening part of Genesis, which fascinated him, and which reveal his keen scientific spirit of enquiry, and also his own dissatisfaction with the incomplete answers to his questioning. Augustine's genius remains unique within the long history of Christianity, and it is little wonder that his influence has been so profound and creative throughout the Western Middle Ages and beyond. My own studies have proved to be a veritable pilgrimage in the footsteps of some of Augustine's ablest disciples: St Gregory the Great, Alcuin, St Anselm and St Bonaventure. Through each of these fathers it is always possible to learn much about the mind of Augustine.

In 1997, I was invited to a monastic conference in Rome and Camaldoli to mark the 1400th anniversary of the coming of St Augustine to Canterbury. It was a unique and happy occasion and the beginning of an important friendship with the Camaldolese Benedictines, as well as many other happy encounters with the Catholic Church in Italy. They have the care of the church and monastery of San Gregorio al Celio in Rome, which St Gregory founded and from which St Augustine came to England. We visited there often with our children, who also went there on their own as students. It is a wonderful place from which to explore the many lovely ancient churches nearby, the catacombs and the Appian Way.

St Gregory the Great is the spiritual father of all English-speaking Christians, Catholics and Anglicans alike. His stature as a pope remains unique and outstanding as "the servant of the servants of Christ", and his pastoral and spiritual influence on all subsequent church life in the West has been profound and long-lasting. He faced a deteriorating situation in Italy in his own lifetime; but he still found the energy and determination to organize the mission to England, which laid the foundations of the English Church. His many writings, which drew upon the theology of Augustine, along with his popularization of the memory of St Benedict and his *Rule* determined the ethos of Western monasticism. A place can convey the spirit of a person, and San Gregorio al Celio is a church where the sense of Gregory's presence is strong and abiding: in the corner is the site of his cell and also his marble chair. No priest can ever lose heart if they remember the wisdom and loving-kindness of this great saint.

Camaldoli too is a special and holy place, in the beautiful forests of the Casentino in the Apennine mountains between Arezzo and Florence. Formed in the tenth century by St Romuald, it combines the eremitic vocation with life in a regular Benedictine monastic community. The hermitages are ringed by an enclosing wall high up in the forest above the monastery itself. The earliest monks were also missionaries in Eastern

Europe and elsewhere, some of them dying as martyrs. After the Schism, they maintained contacts with the Eastern Church; and they also played a formative role in nurturing the thought and art of the early Renaissance in Italy. Today there are Camaldolese communities of men and women across the world—in Italy itself and in France, in Tanzania, and also in North and South America. Their ethos is contemplative, and their ministry includes teaching Scripture to the laity, while cultivating and promoting the monastic art of *lectio divina*.

St Anselm, who came from Aosta in Italy, was one of the most brilliant of Augustine's disciples. In Oxford, I got to know Sir Richard Southern, whose work on the life and theology of Anselm is an exemplary study that fully demonstrates and vindicates the work of a Church historian. He set me on the path of reading Anselm, and his writings have been a constant companion ever since. Two places in particular mediate the reality and memory of the saint: his burial place in the lovely Romanesque chapel in Canterbury Cathedral; and his monastery at Le Bec-Hellouin in Normandy where he was abbot. Anselm was a reluctant Archbishop of Canterbury, however, sometimes in exile on the Continent while he grappled with the two difficult sons of William the Conqueror, William Rufus and Henry I. His life was recounted by his English chaplain, Eadmer, and it is probably the most vivid and outstanding life of a saint ever written in the Middle Ages. As an intellectual theologian, Anselm was without a peer, and his confidence in examining Christian belief without explicit recourse to earlier theologians was remarkable. His *Proslogion* and his prayers exerted a profound influence on Christian thought and prayer for several centuries, being marked by great clarity, sensitivity and insight. His wisdom as a teacher and his fidelity as a friend come across in his many letters, and as a result he is one of those people whom to encounter is never to forget.

I was prompted to discover St Bonaventure, who was born in Bagnoregio near Orvieto, by the theology of Cardinal Ratzinger, the late Pope Benedict XVI, whose visit to England and sermons made a deep impression on me. Like so many people in England, both Catholics and Anglicans, I knew little about Bonaventure, associating him with Aquinas and scholastic theology in the thirteenth century. Encountering Bonaventure has been a transforming experience during the fourth decade of my ministry as a priest.

Bonaventure lived in the thirteenth century and died in 1274 while attending the Second Council of Lyons as a cardinal bishop. The medieval core of his birthplace, Bagnoregio near Orvieto, remains perched on a pinnacle of land left intact after an earthquake. He was educated at the University of Paris where he became a Franciscan and taught theology. In 1257, he was elected as Minister General of the Franciscans, which was a full-time occupation as he trekked the length and breadth of Europe on foot. He continued to write, and also to teach in Paris, where he played a leading role in defending the traditional Augustinian approach to Christian theology, and in challenging the pretensions of philosophy derived from the thought of Aristotle.

After his death, the memory of Bonaventure was partially occluded by the rise of Thomism in the Catholic Church and by the repudiation of scholastic theology by many of the Reformers during the Reformation. The rediscovery of the distinctive ethos of Bonaventure's theology in the twentieth century has had a considerable influence on leading Catholic theologians like Romano Guardini, Hans Urs von Balthasar, and Joseph Ratzinger in the years leading up to and since Vatican II. One of the most enriching aspects of the study of Bonaventure has been to read remarkable studies of him from across Europe and America, and to make new friends who understand and value the unique significance of his spiritual theology, notably a community of Poor Clares in Lovere in northern Italy.

Why is Bonaventure so important? Primarily because he is the most Christ-centred theologian. For him Christ and his death on the Cross is the key to understanding reality, human nature and the whole purpose of God. His theology is steeped in the Bible, and it was considerably influenced by the thinking of Anselm, with whom he had an obvious intellectual and spiritual affinity. Bonaventure was a true disciple of Augustine, but he was also a creative interpreter of his thought, applying it to the novel situation in which he lived and taught, in Paris and elsewhere. Bonaventure's thought is profoundly marked by the memory of St Francis and also of St Clare, and his *Life of St Francis* was commissioned as the definitive life of the saint. The last book for which he was responsible, called *Collations on the Hexaëmeron* or *Illuminations of the Church*, is comparable in its depth and scope to Augustine's *City of God*.

The Franciscans in America have done a great work in translating and publishing most of Bonaventure's writings in English, and it was his *Commentary on St Luke's Gospel* that was my own starting point. I had taught this Gospel for many years to my pupils as Chaplain of Marlborough College, and it was fascinating and enriching to work through the detailed and extensive commentary that Bonaventure wrote to assist the Franciscans in their preaching. Central to his commentary is his very full discussion of the meaning of the Transfiguration. I wrote a book distilling the key themes of Bonaventure's approach to this well-known and well-loved Gospel, which led me on to writing an introductory guide to his spiritual theology, as well as another book examining his last major work, the *Collations on the Hexaëmeron*, in some detail. These books are now being published in Korean to assist the growing life of the Church in South Korea.

One theme that emerges clearly throughout Bonaventure's writings is the Christian vocation to *deification*—being made like Christ in his life and in his death, here and hereafter—and this is the subject of my fourth study of his spiritual theology. In the light of the stigmata of St Francis, Bonaventure perceived that *deiformity*, as he called it in Latin, means *cruciformity*: even as St Paul said, "I have been crucified with Christ." All Bonaventure's spiritual writings and his many sermons are designed to enable Christians to follow the narrow and afflicted path of the Cross, trodden by Francis and Clare, that alone leads to eternal life. He is one of the wisest and most humane of spiritual fathers, a great communicator and pastor, endowed with a very positive vision of what human beings can become when their lives are filled and transformed by the indwelling of the Holy Spirit.

3

# Alfonso de Zulueta

*The Mother of God*

I first met Father Alfonso de Zulueta at lunch at St Benet's Hall in Oxford when I was an Anglican ordinand reading theology at Christ Church. We formed a firm friendship and he generously entertained me on many occasions at his home in Chelsea, where he was Rector of the Catholic Church of St Thomas More in Cheyne Row. We had some very congenial and amusing lunches together at the Chelsea Arts Club, sometimes discussing the significance of St Thomas More. He kindly came to read the epistle at our wedding in Bosham church in September 1977. We kept in regular touch until his death in Spain in 1980, which we only heard about by chance while on holiday in Austria. Father Alfonso was one of the most highly regarded preachers at that time in the English Catholic Church, and his advice to me about preaching has always stood me in good stead, not least when addressing hundreds of teenagers in the Chapel of Marlborough College as their Chaplain: "As you go to preach, just say to yourself: 'Stand up, Speak up, and Shut up!'—and you will." The gracious reply of Cardinal Basil Hume to my letter of condolence was like so many of his kind letters, a blessing and a real encouragement.

Father Alfonso was the fifth Count of Torre Diaz in Spain and came from a distinguished Basque family, some of whom had found refuge in England in the second part of the nineteenth century. They founded a bank and gave generous support to the Catholic Church in London, notably to the church of St James, Spanish Place, as well as making important contributions to public life in the twentieth century. One of their relatives was Cardinal Rafael Merry del Val, who served as Cardinal Secretary of State to Pope Pius X. The beautiful Lady Chapel of St James, Spanish Place, is a fitting and moving memorial to the deep piety of Father Alfonso's family, as well as to his own devotion to their memory.

The first work of Catholic theology that I read as a teenager was Pope St John XXIII's *Journal of a Soul*. This made a deep impression on me, but until I met Father Alfonso in 1976, my only real contact with the Catholic Church had been to visit some of the great monasteries of Lower Austria—Melk, Lilienfeld and Heiligenkreuz—while staying with a devout Protestant family in St Pölten, whose children became firm and lifelong friends. I remember being deeply moved, not so much by the elaborate Baroque architecture, but rather by time spent in the libraries of those monasteries, and also in their quiet and beautiful cloisters. The kindness of the monks I met made a deep impression on me, as did some of the medieval manuscripts that they showed me, a few of which dated back to the time of the English missionaries to the Continent in the eighth century. To handle a virtually contemporary copy of some of Bede's scientific writing in the ornate library of Melk Abbey was an unforgettable experience. It was also a challenging one—how could the links between our churches then have been so close and deep? What had the Church of England lost at the Dissolution of the Monasteries?

It was Father Alfonso who introduced to me the spacious homeliness of the Catholic Church, both as an older friend and also as a fine priest. In a quiet way he prepared me for ordination, setting high standards that were always humane and encouraging, and that were encapsulated in his firm instruction that a priest should never seek preferment. The traumas of the Reformation were not permitted to cloud our friendship, and there was much to learn about the significance of the Mass, the meaning of celibate vocation to the priesthood in the Catholic Church, and also about true devotion to the Blessed Virgin Mary. Father Alfonso was a committed member of The Ecumenical Society of the Blessed Virgin, and he firmly believed that drawing close to Mary spiritually is of vital importance for deepening and strengthening relationships between Christians of different traditions. He also had a strong friendship with Archbishop Michael Ramsey. Father Alfonso taught by his own gracious example, which was rooted in the long-standing Catholic piety of his family throughout many centuries, in England and in Spain.

In my two curacies I was able to form good working friendships with the local Catholic clergy, and as Chaplain of Marlborough College I worked closely with the Catholic parish priests and the Bishops of Clifton in the care of Catholic pupils and in their preparation for Confirmation. It was Father Alfonso who had put me at ease in the Catholic Church and who encouraged me to read Catholic theology and spiritual writing. His preparation also stood me in good stead when I went as a guest of Cardinal Vincentius of Kaunas in Lithuania in 1994. He was a friend of Pope St John Paul II and had endured over twenty years under house arrest as a bishop during the long Communist dictatorship. I was the first Anglican that he had ever entertained, and it was a great privilege to witness the devotion of his people in the cathedral of Kaunas, as he celebrated 50 years as a Catholic priest since his ordination in 1944.

Cardinal Vincentius treated me with every kindness and enabled me to see with his chaplain a great deal of the Catholic Church in that country, including the Hill of Crosses near Siauliai, which had been a place of courageous resistance to Communist rule. This visit was a window into the deep suffering of the Catholic Church in Europe and its tenacious fidelity to the Christian faith. Under the leadership of the cardinal, his energetic restoration of Church life was providing steady leadership and hope to a fledgling democratic society. A most memorable and moving encounter in Lithuania was the sight of a weeping statue of the Madonna set up in a half-built new church in the middle of a rather grim housing estate: a sign of hope in the midst of sorrow and hardship. Some years later I was able to revisit Lithuania to conduct a retreat for Latvian Lutheran clergy at a small Franciscan monastery deep in the snow-bound forests. It was an encouraging sign that the labours of the old cardinal had not been in vain.

Every time I sit in the Lady Chapel of St James, Spanish Place, I realize that it was Father Alfonso who gently introduced to me to the living presence of the Blessed Virgin Mary as the Mother of the Church. As a boy, I used often to go with my father to another lovely Catholic church, St Etheldreda's, Ely Place, which was very near where he worked. Originally it was the chapel of the Bishops of Ely in the Middle Ages, and it was only restored to Catholic worship in 1878. It is dedicated to some of the Catholic martyrs of the Reformation in London and it is a place of quiet beauty and dignity, with amazing modern stained-glass windows. In both these churches, the atmosphere of worship and devotion is palpable, as is so often the quiet presence of the Blessed Virgin Mary herself. The tragedy of the Reformation blinded so many Anglicans and other Protestants to the reality of her prayerful presence in the life of the Church. During my own lifetime and ministry, however, there has been a welcome shift of perception, and there is now a better appreciation in the Church of England of the role of Mary within the worshipping life and prayer of the whole Church.

It was Pope St John Paul II who said that as a priest he had always sensed and relied upon the friendship of the Mother of the Lord, during the hard years of Communist oppression and also as pope. He set a commanding example to any young priest growing up during his primacy. Once again it was Father Alfonso who explained to me the realities surrounding the position of the pope, cutting through the pomp, prejudice and clericalism that so often obscures the essential character of the papal ministry in the life of the Church. This was revealed most memorably when the late Pope Francis stood alone in the wet and windswept piazza in front of St Peter's Basilica to address the world with a pastoral message of hope in the teeth of the Covid crisis in 2020. Perhaps Father Alfonso's most important legacy to me was to enable a sympathetic and respectful understanding of the unique mission of the Catholic Church throughout the world, and of the Blessed Virgin Mary in sustaining it, and also to feel at home whenever I attend the Mass.

So it was that I also often experienced the quiet presence of the Virgin Mary as a companion along my road of being a priest, sometimes at Evensong in my own study. When we lost a baby, she was there for us both in a way that redeemed our sorrow and pledged the wellbeing of our child now in her care. After my mother died, who had sadly become estranged from us due to long-term mental illness, I returned to Austria to visit my friends in St Pölten. I made a pilgrimage by train to Mariazell, a shrine nearby in the mountains above the Danube. On earlier visits as a teenager and before the fall of Communism, I had always been intrigued by the large votive candles representing the lost provinces of the Hapsburg Empire, then behind the Iron Curtain. On this occasion, as I sat in the cemetery above the church, the sense of the presence of the Mother of the Lord was immediate, real and reassuring. On another occasion, sitting in a hermit's cave at Simonos Petra on the Holy Mountain of Athos, her presence was again real, in company with her own Son. The most abiding impression then was of their poverty and simplicity, bearing the sorrows of the world. How could such a mother and her child not be cherished and loved?

The great monastery of Vatopedi on Mount Athos is a pre-eminent Orthodox shrine of the Mother of God—the *Theotokos*. It contains several miracle-working icons, and among its relics is the Girdle of the Virgin Mary, which came from Constantinople via Serbia to the monastery in the Middle Ages. The prayers of this monastery and of the Mother of the Lord through this sacramental relic support a worldwide ministry of healing and blessing for women, often enabling the birth of children in situations that were otherwise without hope. My first impression as a visitor to Vatopedi was of a strong feminine presence and fragrance, in the guest house, and also in the beautiful tenth-century Katholikon—the principal church of the monastery, resplendent with its early medieval mosaics and frescoes, richly decorated and with beautifully conducted liturgy. In the narthex and to the side of the main entrance there is a gracious mosaic of the Virgin Mary responding to the Angel Gabriel, whose mosaic is on the other side of the doorway, as the church and monastery are dedicated to the Annunciation. At this feast, hundreds of pilgrims fill the church and monastery. Such was the skill of the medieval artist that the eyes of the Virgin seem to glint with tears. Deep in the side passages of the Katholikon, and also within its sanctuary, there are ancient icons of the Mother of God that convey a sharp sense of her presence and of her searching compassion. It is impossible not to be moved to compunction by such a loving presence, which challenges and blesses so many lives, near and far.

The most daunting and holy icon of all on Mount Athos is in the sanctuary of the tenth-century Protaton church at Karyes, which is the administrative centre of the Holy Mountain. This icon, called *Axion Estin*, is the palladium of the Athonite community, dating from the tenth century and associated with the angelic gift at that time of the lovely Orthodox prayer of greeting to the Virgin Mary: "It is truly right to call you blessed, who gave birth to God the Word: ever blessed and most pure, and Mother of our God." Once in Nicosia in Cyprus, hard by the Green Line dividing the city, we were visiting a parish church in which there were numerous old icons, some of them rescued from desecrated churches in the Turkish zone of occupation. One in particular commanded my attention: it was of the Mother of God and clearly very old, as you could still see the various levels of its painted surfaces. Suddenly the depth of the original eye caught my eye—penetrating, deeply sorrowful, and yearning with love: a tragic but redeeming presence in a place of unresolved conflict. Yet her presence is not always sorrowful: for example, once while walking on the old cobbled mule track running along the coast near Vatopedi, in the spring when it is strewn with tiny star-shaped white flowers, the coming of the Mother of God was as the loving and joyful herald of the resurrection, of Him who makes all things new. For Athos is truly the Garden of the Virgin Mary.

More recently I have had the privilege of being welcomed by the Carthusian community in Sussex for private retreats in Advent. Their worship is deeply contemplative and unadorned, and the consecration prayer at the Mass is said in silence. The Night Office lasts two hours and uses very large antiphoners full of plainchant in Latin, while the psalms and readings are in English. The darkness between the various sections of the Night Office is deeply moving, as is the profound silence in the chapel. The community lives as hermits in individual houses and they normally only come together for Mass, Vespers, and the Night Office at 12.30 a.m. Their mode of life and prayer is little changed from its inception in the time of St Bruno, their founder, in the eleventh century. Their motto is *Stat Crux dum volvitur Orbis*—"the Cross stands while the world turns". Their devotion to the Blessed Virgin Mary accompanies each office of the day said at set times in their own cells, and her hidden presence there may be sensed in the great silence of the place. The Carthusians are a living link with the first millennium of monastic life and worship in the West. They are also witnesses to terrible persecution on the Continent, and also, alas, in England at the Reformation, when their order was viciously suppressed by Henry VIII. Theirs is therefore a living martyrdom of faithful and hidden prayer, and their witness is now worldwide.

4

# Michael Ramsey

*The Anglican inheritance*

Michael Ramsey was the Archbishop of Canterbury when I was growing up as a teenager and student. He made a habit of coming to preach at least once a year somewhere in Oxford, and it was fascinating to watch him in action answering questions from undergraduates, as he had a great love for young people. His sermons were always cogent and clear; he was a great ambassador for Christianity and also for the priesthood. I have no doubt that it was his example that helped me to decide to become a priest myself in the Church of England. I little thought that circumstances at Cuddesdon outside Oxford, where I went to train and he retired in 1974, would so throw us together that we became firm friends, despite the great difference in our ages. Cuddesdon as a seminary had lost its way, however, despite its distinguished inheritance, and it was not a happy place, either for him during his retirement there, nor for me.

It was an instructive experience, nonetheless. The most valuable part of being there was getting to know Michael Ramsey and to benefit from his wisdom, knowledge and spiritual guidance. He made me very much at home in his study, and we often took long walks through the lovely countryside surrounding the place: he was a true friend.

After he and his wife departed for Durham, we kept in close touch, and his many letters, though almost indecipherable, were always most kind and encouraging. He graciously agreed to marry us in Bosham church near Chichester in September 1977, and he and Lady Ramsey welcomed us to their homes in Durham on several occasions. After his death in 1988, Lady Ramsey, living in Oxford, proved a great friend to our young children as well as to ourselves. They set a fine example of a happy Christian marriage, and it was a privilege and blessing to have known them. Michael Ramsey taught as much by his silence and example as by what he said. He was a highly able person, though very shy. He had a sure grasp of Christian doctrine and a mastery of the Bible, both of which he always brought to life by his clarity and wit. He made it quite apparent that being a Christian priest and theologian was a wonderful vocation and full of interest. He married theology to his prayers, and for him both were rooted in the living past of Christian sanctity and belief. He once defined a saint as someone who makes God real to others, and this was certainly true of him as a priest, a scholar and a friend.

One of my most abiding memories is listening to Michael Ramsey preach about St Anselm in Canterbury Cathedral where we were attending an international Anselm Conference. Sir Richard Southern leant across during the sermon to express his admiration for the archbishop's intimate knowledge of Anselm's letters, which at that time were not yet published in an English translation. For Michael Ramsey, Anselm was perhaps the most important of his predecessors, and he shared this affinity with Pope Paul VI, with whom he forged a strong friendship and who honoured him with the gift of his own episcopal ring, given to him when he was Archbishop of Milan. Michael Ramsey greatly respected Anselm's ability to elucidate Christian belief by using reason in dialogue with Scripture, and he found in Anselm's *Proslogion* and prayers an abiding source of comfort and inspiration. Anselm was an able and well-loved teacher, and this affinity with the young, which comes across in many of his letters, and also in the memories of his friends and disciples, was something to which Michael Ramsey warmed. Like Anselm, he did not take the pomp of his position too seriously, but he had a keen sense of his solemn vocation and duty as archbishop when it came to expounding Christian truth and, if need be, standing up for it. Indeed, Michael Ramsey once said to me that the force of Becket's dilemma as archbishop in confronting the demands of Henry II only really made sense to him when he served as Archbishop of Canterbury himself.

Eadmer, the English biographer of Anselm, paints a vivid and intimate portrait of a very gifted and unusual person, an unwilling bishop in some ways, but a person of great moral courage and intellectual rigour. Anselm was someone who could make God near and real; in his writings he always pointed beyond himself to the greatness and mystery of God, to whom the human heart and mind are drawn by loving thought and prayer.

Michael Ramsey believed it was highly significant that, in the face of the terrible Black Death in the fourteenth century, a group of mystics grew up in England, whose teachings and writings in Middle English he greatly valued and commended. They emerged from the strong anchorite tradition in the medieval Church, the most notable example of whom was Christina of Markyate, who died around the year 1161. The earliest of these fourteenth-century writers was Richard Rolle, whose writings exerted a wide and abiding influence. He lived in Yorkshire, studied at Oxford, and ended his life as Archdeacon of Durham. The rest of his life remains obscure, however, and he died in 1349. His vocation as a spiritual figure and as a hermit was expressed in his many writings for lay men and women, whose lives were outside the monastic orbit. He was well read but very down to earth in his teaching and advice.

The most famous text to emerge from this circle was *The Cloud of Unknowing*, whose writer knew the work of Rolle and who was the most original spiritual writer in the English language at that time. Michael Ramsey rated this as foremost among all mystical texts that teach Christian contemplative prayer. This treatise is surrounded by other works from this unknown writer, who had imbibed the teaching of Dionysius as it had been mediated to medieval Christians by St Bonaventure and others. It seems to have been written between 1345 and 1386, and its writer was probably a priest with a sympathy for the eremitic life and possibly influenced by the Carthusians, or perhaps he was a Dominican solitary himself. His writing sprang from his own spiritual experience, which gives it an abiding authenticity, while at the same time revealing a rich inheritance from earlier writers on the spiritual life, such as Richard of St Victor, Augustine and Gregory the Great, as well as the Carthusian tradition. His work is highly traditional, and it assumes regular participation in the sacramental life of the Church. *The Cloud of Unknowing* ends with these moving words which encapsulate its wisdom: "God sees with His merciful eyes not what you are, nor what you have been, but what you would be." For the consecration of the will lies at the heart of all Christian discipleship and contemplative prayer.

Michael Ramsey also used and commended *The Scale of Perfection* by Walter Hilton as a fine and measured distillation of medieval spiritual tradition. Hilton was probably an Augustinian canon in Nottinghamshire, who died in 1396, but before he became professed he had lived as a hermit for a while. He was a contemporary of William Langland, the author of *Piers Plowman*, and also of the unknown author of the Middle English masterpiece *The Pearl*. Walter Hilton aimed to sum up traditional teaching about the life of prayer while rooting it in very practical and simple language. He painted the life of Christian prayer as a long pilgrimage towards the Kingdom of God, with all its ups and downs and with no short-cuts nor evasion of "nights" of spiritual darkness. In the process, a human person is gradually being transformed by the renewal of their mind and the work of divine grace. He says that "this is only through God's grace stirring the soul, bringing it first into darkness and then into light: . . . for He does it all: He forms and He reforms it." His piety was deeply evangelical, but it assumed a steady commitment to the sacraments of the Church. His writings had a great influence in the fifteenth century up to the time of the Reformation, and *The Scale of Perfection* was printed for the first time in 1494.

The other great spiritual figure from this period of English history is Julian of Norwich, whose writings have become well known in recent times. She was born in 1343 and lived in Norwich, where in later life she became a recluse living by the church of St Julian within the city; she was still alive in 1416. By this time, she exercised a wide ministry of spiritual counsel, and she was visited by Margery Kempe sometime in the first decade of the fifteenth century. In 1373, during a severe illness, she received a series of "showings" from God, which are now preserved in two versions, short and long.

Formed within the later medieval tradition of devotion to the Cross and to the sufferings of Christ and his holy Mother, Julian sought to experience participation in these mysteries, and this desire came to a head during her illness in which she nearly died. Her writings need to be read carefully, as they mediate a remarkable vision of God's grace revealed in Jesus Christ by which she lived and prayed for the rest of her life. Michael Ramsey valued them greatly for their feminine sensitivity, clarity and humble good sense.

Julian drew close in particular to the terrible sufferings of Mary as the Mother of Jesus: "For Christ and she were so united in love that the greatness of her loving was the cause of the greatness of her pain." She sensed that Mary is the Mother of all human beings, having become the Mother of the Saviour, who Himself is "our very own Mother". The gift of the Eucharist is the way in which Christ nourishes the soul: "For our precious Mother, Jesus, feeds us with Himself, full courteously and full tenderly." For Julian in the end, "Love is His meaning." Julian's deep sensibility thus quietly helped to transform one of the most important strands of spiritual insight in the Middle Ages, which can be traced back to the spiritual legacy of Anselm and the teaching of Bonaventure. Her writings, along with those of Walter Hilton, were fortunately preserved by Catholic émigrés on the Continent, who had fled the Reformation in England, and they were commended by Father Augustine Baker and other Benedictines in the seventeenth century.

This important spiritual legacy persuaded Michael Ramsey that the emergence of the Anglican Church as a result of the upheavals of the Reformation and the murky politics of England was deeply rooted in the *Ecclesia Anglicana* of the medieval period. In the writings of Richard Hooker, Lancelot Andrewes and other Anglican divines there was a real and conscious continuity with the medieval inheritance. Some of the roots of Puritanism also lay in the Lollard movement of the fifteenth century and in the teaching of Wycliffe, who was himself an heir to a strong tradition of independent thought and critique stretching back to Robert Grosseteste, a bishop of Lincoln in the thirteenth century, and to the arrival of the Franciscans in 1224. *The Pilgrim's Progress* by John Bunyan was also a direct beneficiary of popular medieval piety and saints' lives, cast in the dress of the seventeenth century, and engaging with the moral and spiritual challenges of the day. The writings of Thomas Traherne and the other poets of that century, like George Herbert, were eloquent witnesses to this vital English spiritual tradition.

Michael Ramsey conveyed strongly and in a memorable way the sense that the present life of the Church of England is set within a living past—the communion of its saints. For him, this reality was mediated by the strong memory of three great Anglican bishops of modern times: Edward King, Charles Gore and William Temple, the last two of whom he encountered and remembered personally. Being brought up as a nonconformist and evangelical, Michael Ramsey maintained a healthy detachment towards the Anglican establishment, but as an heir of the Tractarians he was eager to strengthen the apostolic and catholic character of the Church of England. His ecumenical experience, which was extensive and significant, especially as Archbishop of Canterbury, placed this conviction within a worldwide perspective.

Edward King was Bishop of Lincoln, and he died in 1910. He was the first Tractarian bishop, and he suffered opposition and criticism for his renewal of liturgical life and ritual. He embodied the spirit of Cuddesdon in the early period of its existence, having served there firstly as chaplain and then, after a crisis, as its principal. From there he went to be a canon of Christ Church, Oxford, and Professor of Pastoral Theology in the university. His influence on a whole generation of clergy and others was profound and long-lasting, and his work as an active pastoral bishop in the vast and impoverished Diocese of Lincoln left an abiding memory of sanctity. Michael Ramsey often spoke warmly about him as a role model for any priest or bishop and he sensed in him a kindred spirit. Edward King was in the same mould as his great Carthusian predecessor, St Hugh of Lincoln, who died in 1200.

Charles Gore was perhaps the most intellectually outstanding of the later Victorian bishops who assumed a prophetic stature by his forceful preaching and fearless writing. Michael Ramsey often heard him preach at Westminster Abbey and elsewhere, after he resigned his bishopric in 1919 to undertake the renewal of Christian belief in the aftermath of the First World War, by writing *The Reconstruction of Belief*, and also to pursue ecumenical contacts with the Orthodox church in Romania and elsewhere. He was an energetic Bishop of Worcester, who created the see of Birmingham and became its first bishop in 1905. Then in 1911 he was translated to the see of Oxford, which brought him closer to some of the confusing currents of thought then beginning to assail the Church of England. He was a devotee of the Book of Common Prayer and critical of ritualist tendencies among the Anglo-Catholics. Before he became a bishop, Gore had served as a canon of Westminster Abbey with a commanding preaching ministry. Before that he created the Community of the Resurrection, a community of priests bound by vows, first at Radley near Oxford, and finally at Mirfield in Yorkshire. His critical and historical approach to classical Christian doctrine and the Bible was encapsulated in the publication of *Lux Mundi* in 1889. Michael Ramsey saw himself very much as an heir and beneficiary of Gore's teaching and also of his approach to pastoral ministry as a bishop; he always spoke to me warmly of Gore and encouraged me to take his theology seriously.

William Temple exerted a formative influence on Michael Ramsey as a young priest, and his memory informed his own approach to being Archbishop of Canterbury. William Temple served as Bishop of

Manchester and then as Archbishop of York, and he was responsible for major initiatives in the inter-war period, addressing the chronic social and economic problems of the country which helped to lay the basis for the welfare state that was created after the end of the Second World War. His keen social conscience was something shared by Charles Gore and later Michael Ramsey, and it sprang from deep belief in the significance of the Incarnation for understanding the real value of human life. Unlike Gore and Ramsey, Temple was a philosopher before he became an active theologian, and his confidence in human reason and the transforming spirit of the gospel sustained his extraordinary range of endeavours as a bishop. Like Gore, he was committed to ecumenical relationships, forging many friendships of importance across the world.

William Temple's premature death in 1944 as Archbishop of Canterbury was a serious loss not only to the Anglican Church worldwide and England in particular, but also to the moral leadership of the Western world as it emerged from the wreckage of the war. All that Michael Ramsey sought to achieve as Archbishop of Canterbury was measured in his mind by the memory of Temple, and he was able, in conversation and in his own writings, to bring bishops like King, Gore and Temple to life by his well-informed appreciation of their legacy and spiritual significance. He believed that Anglicanism is an authentic expression of catholic and orthodox Christianity, with a deep and strong spiritual tradition rooted in the Incarnation, and that this is its true foundation in every generation.

I set my hand to write a study of Michael Ramsey's spiritual theology called *Glory: The Spiritual Theology of Michael Ramsey* in time for the centenary of his birth in 2004, which was celebrated by various people, including myself, in places associated with his ministry and memory. This book was intended to complement the magisterial biography of him that was written by his friend, Owen Chadwick. Michael Ramsey left his mark on my own ministry as a priest and teacher in so many ways. It was his generous friendship and spiritual stature that made an abiding and formative impression on my own prayers and conduct of divine worship. Indeed, every time I celebrate the Eucharist, especially when using the Book of Common Prayer, I remember how he celebrated, and the simple holiness that radiated from his devotion. When I preach, I always remember his witty advice to "preach the Gospel as someone may just be listening!". For him, priesthood was the heart of the matter, even as a bishop; his character was marked by humble self-sacrifice and reverence towards the awesome reality and holiness of God and the deep mystery of Calvary. He was the most Christ-centred person I have ever met, someone in whom the fire of the Holy Spirit burned, and from whom it reached out to raise the morale of the clergy and to transform the lives of all those who came to know and love him.

5

# Benedicta Ward

*History and hagiography*

I first met Sister Benedicta Ward at a lecture given by Dom Jean Leclerq to the Stubbs Historical Society in Christ Church, Oxford, in February 1973, and this was followed by a further encounter with her at a seminar conducted by her mentor Sir Richard Southern later that year, also in Oxford. She invited me to visit her at her home, Fairacres, a convent of contemplative Anglican nuns in Oxford called the Sisters of the Love of God. In this way, a firm friendship was born, with her and also with this remarkable monastic community, for my wife and myself, that has lasted for over fifty years since we were both students. She was also an active godmother to our children.

Sister Benedicta's most outstanding achievement was to translate and publish the prayers and meditations of St Anselm in a definitive version that is unlikely to be superseded. She also wrote a notable study of miracles in the medieval mind, but she is perhaps most widely known abroad for her translations of the sayings of the Desert Fathers and Mothers from the earliest era of Christian monasticism. She was an active participant in many conferences and publishing projects, all the while continuing the life of a contemplative nun with the support of her community, while also teaching in the University of Oxford. Sister Benedicta embodied the monastic vocation with simplicity, sincerity and grace, and also made its relevance immediately accessible and instructive. She was a great person of prayer, faithful and assiduous in her spiritual care of others, and endowed with a gift of friendship for so many who encountered her: she blessed many lives.

When I decided not to become an Anglican priest within the context of university life but rather to train as a parish priest, Sister Benedicta was a constant support and interlocutor, who enabled me to maintain my studies and research into Anglo-Saxon church history throughout many years. She demonstrated the viability of Christian scholarship outside the formal structures of university and seminary, and also its crucial importance for the wider life and integrity of the Church. A Church historian has a particular vocation, and the field of Anglo-Saxon studies is a rich one, where archaeology continually corroborates the written evidence that still remains. It is a long period of history, stretching over four hundred years, from the coming of St Augustine to Canterbury in 597 to the Norman Conquest in 1066.

I did not initially warm to medieval studies, however, while reading Modern History at Oxford, but the lectures of Professor Henry Mayr Harting and Sir Richard Southern opened my eyes. I deliberately marked the beginning of my ordination training by obtaining a reprint of Stubbs' *Memorials of St Dunstan*, which he had published as part of the Rolls Series in the nineteenth century. I had known about St Dunstan since childhood, as my father had been a pupil at St Dunstan's College in London where I was also educated; otherwise, I had only a sketchy understanding of his significance. Before leaving Oxford in 1977, I collected together many of the primary resources that I needed for continuing my research while serving in a parish as a curate. Fortunately, the two incumbents with whom I trained were generously sympathetic and encouraging towards this project.

Very little of the remaining primary material from that time had been translated from Latin, however, and most of my secondary research was done in the University Library in Cambridge; the internet had not yet been developed. Life as Chaplain at Marlborough College gave me a third of the year in vacation, however, and easy access to Oxford, so I was able to publish the first definitive life of Dunstan in time for his millennium in 1988. This anniversary was also marked by a notable international pilgrimage to England from Anglican and Catholic churches and schools dedicated to St Dunstan across the world in order to visit places associated with him—Glastonbury, Worcester, London and Canterbury. I was able to follow this up in 1989 by an extensive programme of talks, sermons and seminars in various Dunstan churches across the United States. It was remarkable that so distant a figure could command such interest and respect.

To work closely with the life of a saint is a great challenge and a profoundly formative experience. How should five successive *Lives* of Saint Dunstan be assessed, stretching as they did through the traumatic revolution in English church and society caused by the Norman Conquest in 1066? Dunstan left very little written work and only one outline for a work of art, though he was an active scholar, artist and musician. Exploring his life was rather like excavating the Sutton Hoo ship burial: the timbers were long gone, but the impress of the subject was everywhere around to be carefully examined and pieced together. This is exactly true for the life of Dunstan, who as a statesman and churchman was one of the architects of early medieval England, as well as being responsible with others like St Ethelwold and St Oswald for the firm establishment of Benedictine monastic life in the tenth century that would last until the Reformation. The Coronation Order is the abiding legacy of that time, enshrining the all-important Christian principle of accountability under the rule of law. Close study of this formative century raised the question of what is a saint, and how do such figures emerge within a Christian society? How is it possible for such a person to shape a society and its values in the midst of so much turmoil and violence? The murder of St Thomas à Becket undoubtedly obscured the memory of St Dunstan at Canterbury, as did the English Reformation much later with its repudiation of monasticism. But his significance and stature remain as one of the greatest English churchmen.

The English Church is fortunate in having as its first historian the Venerable Bede, and Sister Benedicta Ward was a great authority on him, being steeped in his many theological writings, as well as in his work as an outstanding historian and hagiographer. It seemed to me, however, that there was an unrealistic polarization in many minds between the Celtic and Anglo-Saxon churches, so I took in hand an extensive study that examined the theological background to all the missionary activities of so many notable saints in and from the British Isles, from the time of St Patrick to that of St Boniface. This book was published in time to mark the anniversary in 1997 of the coming of St Augustine to Canterbury in 597, which was also the year in which St Columba died on the island of Iona.

The historical study of Christian hagiography is the art of listening carefully to what the primary texts can tell us about the beliefs of saints and their immediate disciples, and also about how they were perceived and valued more widely in their day. Throughout this study of Christian mission, and by visiting many of the places associated with them, I received and have retained a lively sense of their continuing spiritual reality and significance. The English Church is blessed to have such a rich record of Christian mission, and also such tangible and beautiful evidence of effective acculturation, for example in the Lindisfarne Gospels.

The last decade of my time as Chaplain of Marlborough College was marked by a major research project into the life and works of Alcuin. He was a notable Anglo-Saxon scholar and teacher from York, who went to the Continent at the behest of Charlemagne towards the end of the eighth century. He ended his life as abbot of the monastery of St Martin at Tours. I had no idea about the scale of research that this would entail, but it opened doors to Italian and French scholarship that proved deeply enriching and stimulating. The range of Alcuin's influence and the plethora of his writings, including his many letters, shed a sharp light on a fascinating and important period in European history, one that laid the foundations for subsequent medieval learning and political theory.

One of the privileges of such research was being able to handle original manuscripts from the period in the Bodleian Library in Oxford. This transformed my sense of Scripture in particular, as a written version so carefully executed and often preserved against the odds brings the sacramental character of the Bible very close as pre-eminently a work of prayer. In their day, knowledge of Scripture was the gateway to literacy as well as to prayer itself, something to be learnt and memorized before actually being read, and its transmission and preservation was always a great labour and expense. In the case of Alcuin, because he wrote so much, the sense of his character and presence is very strong; his genius as a framer of liturgy and prayers has left a permanent mark on Western Christianity.

Sister Benedicta Ward also taught me much about the inner ethos of monastic life and contemplative spirituality. She was not perturbed by the manifest difficulties of the Church of England or of the Roman Catholic Church, seeing beneath the turmoil the hidden providence and purpose of God. She was a good and trusted listener, well informed about what was going on, while not herself a participant. Her interest and encouragement were real and constant, even though she herself was by nature quite a shy and reserved person. In her later years, she had to contend with increasing secularization in the teaching of theology in the university, as well as mounting ignorance of monastic life and witness within the life of the modern church.

Sister Benedicta's friendship and encouragement enabled me to form strong friendships with several other nuns, in her community and also elsewhere; and their feminine insight into the meaning of Christianity is something that I have always valued and from which I have greatly benefited. This is particularly true in relation to the Carmelite witness and writings of St Thérèse of Lisieux and especially St Elizabeth of the Trinity, both of whom died very young after serious illness. Their wisdom is rooted in their devout spiritual upbringing within the French Catholic Church at a time of bitter persecution at the end of the nineteenth century. Their vision always remained that of their own childhood, and there is a youthful vitality and clarity about their writings, which speaks directly to the soul and is profoundly transforming, renewing and inspiring. The nurturing of vocations to monastic life is a sign of a healthy Church, and also a vital challenge to the values of an increasingly secular, ignorant and materialistic society. Contemplative prayer brings the continuing spiritual witness of the saints very close indeed, with the keen sense that they pray with us and for us. Each Christian is bidden in their own way to "seek the better part" in response to the loving call of Jesus himself: to seek him and to love him above all else.

One of the most attractive features of Anglo-Saxon church history is the importance of so many holy places that can still be visited in England, often with Bede's *History* in hand, and also, the prominence that he gave to the role of holy women, like Hilda and Etheldreda, in nurturing the life of the English Church in that formative seventh century. The hidden prayer of holy women is a recurrent theme throughout the Anglo-Saxon period, expressed, for example, in wonderful eighth-century prayer books like the *Nunnaminster Codex* and the *Book of Cerne*. Holy women also played a key role in facilitating the revival of monastic life in the tenth century under the leadership of Dunstan.

As a child, a Christian friend of my mother's used to entertain me in her home in Thanet, driving me around in her little green Austin car to visit numerous churches and sites in that part of Kent. The story is told of how my parents once lost me as a little child while they were visiting with her the ruins of the Roman fort and Anglo-Saxon church at Reculver. This is a haunting place, perched on the edge of the sea, and I was found in a trench, talking with an archaeologist! Minster-in-Thanet, associated with St Mildred, is another place lodged in my earliest memory, and the sense of her character and memory has always remained with me, as she made a deep impression on her contemporaries and on the early life of the Church in Kent.

I often visited Canterbury Cathedral as a child, and there, especially in the crypt, and also in the ruins of St Augustine's Abbey, I sensed that something significant had happened there: these are holy places. The unique atmosphere of the Roman church of St Martin in Canterbury, outside the city walls, always conveyed a real sense of the continuity of the Christian past and its mysterious presence. It is the place where Bertha, the Christian queen of Kent, prayed and it became Augustine's first base as a missionary. The very fact that Thanet had once been an island intrigued me greatly as a child, as evidence of the passing of time and the alteration of place, and it was always exciting to be able to catch a glimpse of France across the Channel, as my family never visited the Continent.

Another place which has made a comparable and lasting impression of how Christian history is actually a living spiritual past impinging upon present spiritual life is Durham with its great cathedral, and also the holy island of Lindisfarne. We stayed with Michael Ramsey and his wife in Durham, and he always conveyed a living sense of Aidan, Bede and Cuthbert as spiritually alive as we walked together along the River Wear. They meant a great deal to him, as he and his wife had formed their first home in Durham, and in due time he served as a well-beloved Bishop of Durham. Our children also benefited from our visits to Durham and two of them later became students at the university there.

We often had holidays overlooking Lindisfarne and the Farne Islands, ranging up into the neighbouring hills to explore St Cuthbert's Cave. Boat trips to the Farne Islands to see the seals and the birds were always a vital part of the whole experience. It is there on Inner Farne, and also on Lindisfarne itself among the ruins of its abbey, that the sense of Aidan and Cuthbert becomes very real and deeply moving. Also to kneel in the Galilee Chapel of Durham Cathedral by the tomb of Bede, or by Cuthbert's tomb behind the high altar, is always a deeply moving experience, the humbling sense of being an heir to so rich a tradition of Christian faith and life. It was a privilege to be associated with the dedication of a wonderful window of the Transfiguration in memory of Michael Ramsey that is very close to the tomb of St Cuthbert.

It is possible to experience a rich pilgrimage of faith to places like Lastingham, the cathedrals at Lichfield, Winchester, Worcester, Wells and also York Minster, to name but a few, where evidence of the Anglo-Saxon period of church life is readily evident. Likewise small churches, such as the one at Bradford-on-Avon, or Selham and Bosham in Sussex, or at Escomb near Durham, are just as moving and memorable, as are the larger churches at Jarrow and Monkwearmouth with their tangible associations with Bede, or the great basilica at Brixworth in Northamptonshire. All these and other similar places are important witnesses to the truth so well expressed by T. S. Eliot in the last of his *Four Quartets*: "You are here to kneel where prayer has been valid."

6

# Donald Allchin

*The Vision Glorious*

I first got to know Donald Allchin when he was Warden of the Sisters of the Love of God at Fairacres in Oxford, and our friendship continued during the time that he was a canon at Canterbury Cathedral and then Director of the St Theosevia Centre in Oxford. In due time he retired to Bangor in North Wales to teach at the university there, and our friendship was then sustained mainly by letters. Donald was a true angel of the Lord inasmuch as he had the gift of providing warm friendship at the right moment, and then spurring a person on in their own vocation with renewed vision and enthusiasm. He was indeed an enthusiast, always discovering something new in the Christian tradition, making it his own, and then eager to share it with anyone who would listen. There was indeed "a boundless grandeur" to his spiritual vision, and his energy and memory were quite extraordinary. He was endowed richly with the capacity to take a keen, sympathetic and encouraging interest in others, and he had a genius for forming and sustaining many friendships, far and wide. He embodied the true spirit of ecumenism by recognizing and affirming, and also by learning from, those he encountered from other parts of the Christian Church. For what is Christianity if is not a web of prayerful friendships? For Donald Allchin, these friendships spanned time and space: he was a true believer in the reality of the communion of saints.

Donald Allchin introduced me to the richness of Orthodox theology to be found in the contemporary work of scholars in America and also in Europe. Encountering the theology of Vladimir Lossky transformed my understanding of Christian theology, especially the Incarnation and the Transfiguration, which have since been central to my own study and thought. The visits that we were able to make to Russia as Communism was collapsing confirmed the reality of this vision in the rich and tenacious Orthodox worshipping tradition there, that was expressed in monastic life and also in music and icons. Donald was a sure bridge into Orthodoxy inasmuch as he had a close friendship with Dumitru Stăniloae, the outstanding Romanian theologian, whose theology had been forged in the crucible of persecution and suffering. They were active collaborators when freedom gradually returned to Romania, and as a result Stăniloae's work was steadily translated into English.

At a time when the Church of England appeared uncertain in its own belief in the Incarnation, these and other Orthodox writings were an invaluable corrective and support for many Anglicans, including myself. Donald demonstrated that the truth of Christianity, its orthodox and catholic character, is something deeply real, accessible and attractive. His close friendship with the late Bishop Kallistos Ware was important for them both, and they were able exponents and ambassadors for a large-hearted expression of Orthodoxy, which was rooted in sound patristic scholarship. Bishop Kallistos became a good friend and teacher to me and to so many others, within and beyond the Orthodox Church. The clarity of his learning and the depth of his faith, as well as his kindness and friendship, left a lasting impression.

It was due to Bishop Kallistos' encouragement that the door opened for me to become a regular pilgrim to the Holy Mountain of Athos, to the great and lovely monasteries of Vatopedi and Simonospetra where I have made many friends. The renewal of monastic life on Athos has been one of the quiet miracles of our time, as indeed has been the comparable renewal of monastic life in Egypt and elsewhere, for example in Ukraine. As soon as Communism ended, the Russian Orthodox Church was able to restore monasteries across Russia to an extraordinary extent, and this has also been true in other lands freed from Communist dictatorship, such as Romania. The renewal of Athonite spiritual life had its root in the faithful witness of hermits there, and also in the vitality of the Greek Church after the end of the Second World War.

The writings that have emerged from this monastic renewal on Athos are simple in their profundity: for example, the teaching of the Elder Aimilianos of Simonospetra and Abbot Vasileios of Stavronikita share the wisdom of the Holy Mountain far and wide. Perhaps the most notable development in the post-war period has been renewed interest in and appreciation of the theology of St Gregory Palamas, and I have learnt a great deal about the inner nature of prayer from his writings and the work of Father John Meyendorff. It has been a privilege to be able to share in so many long and moving services on the Holy Mountain, as well as to delight in its beauty and quietness: it is a true school of prayer.

Donald Allchin became a fervent ambassador for Welsh Christianity. He learnt Welsh as an adult and always protested the fact that few English people ever learnt the language. He thought that this blind spot went back a long way to the time of the Anglo-Saxon invasions, when Bede himself promoted in his *Church History* a disparaging attitude towards the British Christian people whom his ancestors were forcibly displacing. Christianity has thrived in Wales since Roman times and the spiritual witness and historic mission of Welsh Christianity has been profoundly formative and influential there and far beyond, initially in Ireland and Brittany, then in modern times across the world in North and South America.

One of the most important things that Donald Allchin achieved was to help draw attention to the remarkable poetry of Ann Griffiths. In the foothills of the beautiful Berwyn Mountains lies the quiet village of Dolanog where in 1805 this young woman, the newly wedded wife of a farmer, died at the age of 30, soon after the birth of their first child, who had also just died. She grew up in a devout Anglican family whose Christian faith was nurtured by the Book of Common Prayer and the Authorised Version of the Bible, both in Welsh. In her early twenties, her faith caught fire as a result of experiencing the evangelical preaching of some early Methodists. Thereafter her spiritual life was shared within a tight-knit local circle of like-minded Christian friends, and it does not seem that Ann ever travelled further than Bala or learnt English. She expressed her spiritual experience in private poems which she shared with her close friend and servant, and occasionally with others.

After Ann's death, the poems were dictated from memory by her friend to her husband, who was a pastor and, thus preserved, some of them were turned into hymns later in the nineteenth century. Then in the twentieth century, the authentic texts were recovered, studied and published as some of the finest poetry ever written in Welsh. What is striking about the poetry of Ann Griffiths is the depth and breadth of her understanding of Christian truth: how could this be in someone without any formal education? It is testimony to the transforming power of Scripture and regular prayer that allows the language of the Holy Spirit to bring wisdom and understanding to a person who is sincerely committed to Christ. Her poetry is indeed "tongued with fire". It is also a tribute to the strong spiritual friendships from which she benefited and which supported her own Christian life.

In another remote and lovely valley not far away under the Berwyn Mountains there once lived a saint, later called Melangell—"Good angel" in Welsh. She was an Irish princess escaping a forced marriage, who took refuge, probably in the seventh century, as a hermit in the valley of Cwm Pennant where the local ruler of Powys found her while out hunting: the hares he was chasing had taken refuge under her skirts. He respected her vocation and gave her his protection, and so a small Christian monastery was formed that by the twelfth century became a place of pilgrimage. At the Reformation, the local people continued to treasure her memory, and her relics were carefully hidden, as were fragments of her elaborately carved shrine. Towards the end of the twentieth century, the church was so neglected that it was almost a ruin, but some Christians came together to restore it. Donald Allchin played a key role in encouraging this venture, and there were sufficient fragments of the early medieval shrine left to enable its careful reconstruction. It now stands in the chancel of the church of Pennant Melangell as a tall stone box in which the saint's relics are lodged, set on elaborate carved pillars and topped by a roof-like structure. It attracts many pilgrims, Anglicans, Catholics and Orthodox, and has become a place of prayer for healing and of spiritual care.

This is a striking example of how a trickle of life-giving love flowed through many centuries, at times almost forgotten, but not quite. What it demonstrates is that in a person truly dedicated to Christ, however obscure, the Holy Spirit can become an indwelling reality that makes God's presence and compassion real—to those around, and also within the continuing memory and praying life of the Church. Time is no inhibiting barrier, for in Christianity the living past of the saints sustains in hidden but palpable ways the living spiritual present of the Church. This is what is meant by the phrase "the Communion of Saints" in the Apostles' Creed. For *Communio Sanctorum* means the communion of holy people, and also holy places that have been transformed by participation in the divine life outpoured in the sacraments of the Church, in Baptism and in the Eucharist, which constitute the fundamental "communion of holy things". Donald always sensed and affirmed the "thinness" that can be sensed in such holy places "where prayer has been valid".

Far away off the tip of the Llyn peninsula lies the awesome island mountain of Bardsey—*Ynys Enlli*—"The Island of 20,000 Saints". A monastery was founded there in the sixth century by St Cadfan, and it became a major goal of pilgrimage in the Middle Ages, despite the hazardous crossing by sea. Ruins of the abbey still remain, and the island is now managed by a trust as a centre for watching birds. For Christians, however, it is also a symbol of, and a memorial to all the saints everywhere, who are "known only unto God". Donald Allchin was active in supporting a number of hermits, some associated with the Sisters of the Love of God, who lived near Aberdaron and in sight of Bardsey Island. Perhaps one of his most significant achievements was to stimulate renewed consideration of the spiritual importance and nature of the eremitic life. Donald's first book was a detailed and original study of the renewal of monastic life within the Church of England in the nineteenth century as the fruit of the Tractarian Movement. An attempt had been made in the 1930s by William of Glasshampton to live as a hermit in Worcestershire, but his example was not followed. Then in 1975 an international conference was held at St David's in Wales to reflect on the revival of eremitic life in parts of the Western and Eastern churches, and to consider its spiritual significance in modern society. This led to the life of a hermit being formally recognized within the Church of England in order to nurture and encourage this hidden witness to the gospel. Once again, Donald was brilliant at conveying the essential spirit of such secluded contemplative life in a way that spoke from the depths of tradition, but also directly to the spiritual aspirations and needs of committed Christians today. St David's remains one of the most important spiritual places in the British Isles, where a sense of holy antiquity is undergirded by primeval geology and wild natural beauty.

Towards the end of his life, Donald Allchin was instrumental in the recovery and publication of the writings of Thomas Traherne. Important parts of these were discovered almost by chance in the library of Lambeth Palace by my fellow-scholar and friend, Jeremy Maule, who sadly died young. Traherne was born in 1637; he went to Brasenose College in Oxford in 1652 aged 15 and graduated in 1656. He was ordained in 1660 as the parish priest of Credenhill in Herefordshire, and he died relatively young in 1674. He was a deeply committed Anglican of the generation that had grown up during the Civil War and which was now engaged in making the restoration of the Church of England a credible reality. Only one of his writings was published in his lifetime, a few after his death; then there was a hiatus during which much of his work appeared to be forgotten and lost. Then some more was published early in the twentieth century, to be followed by a burst of interest prompted by the recovery of more material early in the present century in England and America. As a result, Traherne's stature as a poet and theologian has been restored, and interest in his work abounds in England and America.

Donald Allchin was from the beginning a great enthusiast for Traherne's poetry, frequently commending it, and delighted by the recovery of the manuscripts at

Lambeth and elsewhere. Transfiguration is a central theme in Traherne's spiritual and aesthetic vision, and his eloquence in embracing the rich diversity and beauty of the natural world is matched by an acute knowledge of current scientific developments and their significance. He also addressed quite forcefully controversial issues within the Anglican Church and in its relationships with Protestants and Catholics. Traherne was very well informed, and he is a good example of someone for whom there was an unbreakable union between theology, prayer, and a sensitive perception of the natural world.

Donald Allchin wrote a little book in 1988 called *Participation in God* about the way in which deification is an overlooked strand within Anglican tradition. He showed how belief in this reality lies at the heart of the theology of the great Anglican divines, Richard Hooker and Lancelot Andrewes, and also, in that of Charles Wesley and the Welsh hymnwriter Williams Pantycelyn. From there he outlined its presence in the theology of the Oxford Movement, notably in the writings of Pusey. He was well able to place this deep tradition within the wider perspective of Catholic and Orthodox theology, indicating its evidence in the language of poets like R. S. Thomas. It was a prophetic book, whose vision was richly corroborated by the subsequent rediscovery of the breadth and depth of Traherne's writing, which demonstrate the way in which deification is at the heart of Anglican Christianity. By his own vitality and holiness, Donald embodied and communicated the living reality of deification as the true Christian vocation and the very heart of all prayer, being a bond of loving union with Christ and between Christians everywhere.

7

# Peter Walker

*A bishop's charism*

Peter Walker was a canon of Christ Church and the Bishop of Dorchester near Oxford when I got to know him as an undergraduate. He was a gracious and rather shy person who became a firm friend then and also later, when he invited me to serve my second curacy at the parish church in Ely where he was the bishop. Peter was a true pastor, and this was his greatest strength as a bishop and also in his retirement, when I often used to visit him and his wife, Jean, in Cambridge. He steered me towards becoming a school chaplain, having been one himself for a while, and always took a keen and perceptive interest in my ministry as Chaplain of Marlborough College. He was learned, though very modest about it: his great love was St Augustine whom we often discussed. He once pointed to his set of Augustine texts and said that they reproached him every day for all the distractions that kept him from studying them while serving as a bishop. He thought that scholarship mattered and that Anglicanism has a long and distinguished tradition of it that should be cherished.

Peter Walker was a very good and wise listener, sympathetic but critical, though never uncharitable. He also wrote the most elegant short letters, which were always to the point and often memorable too. By temperament he was reflective, and long pauses would often occur in the middle of conversations and during sermons too. He had a well-cultivated artistic sensibility, owning some wonderful paintings by John Piper and others, and he had a poetic use of language, although at times he could appear *amletico* [i.e. like Hamlet] and indecisive. It was his thoughtfulness and sensitivity to others, and to the various sides of an argument, that held him back from more dogmatic pronouncements, which he always rather abhorred. He was a true servant of the Church of England to which he showed devoted loyalty, and he expected it from others too. His many friendships within what might then still be called "the Establishment" were a source of great interest to him, and this cautioned him and those he advised against any rashness of judgement or impatience with the vagaries of the institution. In a way, Peter Walker was the archetypal "good bishop"—steadfast, unassuming and genuinely kind. He was a person whom people could trust.

He used to say that one of the most formative influences on his own life and ministry was his encounter with Bishop George Bell of Chichester, in whose home he had stayed for a while as a young midshipman. Peter Walker revered George Bell and held him up as an exemplary and prophetic figure. He had no doubts about his great moral integrity and resilience, and also his capacity not to be cowed when in the middle of the Second World War he condemned openly in the House of Lords the wholesale bombing of German cities. This stance did not commend him to the government, however, and it was often said that, when Archbishop William Temple suddenly died in 1944, Bell was passed over as his obvious successor. George Bell had been able to make the case in Parliament that he did because of his own contacts with some in the German Resistance, and also his extensive ecumenical friendships on the Continent in Scandinavia and elsewhere. Before and after the war, Bell was a great protagonist of ecumenical rapprochement, being an energetic letter writer and traveller. As Dean of Canterbury, he had pioneered the performance of music and drama in the cathedral, and after the war he continued to encourage art and music in the life of the cathedral at Chichester. Bell was a man of vision, and although he had been assiduously formed as the chaplain of Archbishop Randall Davidson, whose magisterial biography he wrote, and was a devoted servant of the Church of England, he always remained its critical friend, with an independent turn of mind and a dogged insistence on matters of principle that his fellow peers sometimes found rather wearisome. For Peter Walker, therefore, George Bell was the yardstick by which effective episcopacy could be measured, and he was able to impart a very lively and immediate sense of Bell's character and stature.

My father had encouraged me to read the biographies of Bell, Garbett, Temple and other notable Anglican bishops while I was still at school. Their examples certainly kindled my own sense of vocation and vision of what an Anglican priest or bishop is called to be. They were great statesman and widely respected beyond the confines of the Church of England. Peter Walker helped to bring them to life in a way that imparted something of their keen sense of mission as well as of history. What should a bishop be? What kind of formation is needed to nurture effective church leaders? These questions have accompanied my whole ministry, and meeting many bishops and abbots abroad, Lutheran, Catholic and Orthodox, as well as overseas Anglican bishops, has been fascinating and very instructive too. I have no doubt that effective episcopacy is absolutely essential for the life and mission of the Church.

A bishop must be loving and learned, and able to teach and preach clearly and well by "speaking the truth in love", cherishing the clergy, and ensuring that Christianity is never put on the defensive. I greatly appreciated the friendship of three very fine bishops: Michael Scott-Joynt as Bishop of Winchester; John Kirkham, formerly Bishop of Sherborne and Bishop to the Armed Forces; and Simon Barrington-Ward, formerly Bishop of Coventry, each of whom was very kind to me, offering wise advice and support at various moments in my ministry.

One of the most important of the many friendships that George Bell nurtured was his relationship with the German pastor, Dietrich Bonhoeffer. He was a leading light in the Confessing Church in Germany that resisted the Nazi takeover of the Lutheran state Church. I had known about Bonhoeffer since childhood because the pastor of the church we went to then had known him and worked with him before the war, when Bonhoeffer was pastor of the German church in Sydenham in south London. Reading some of the Bonhoeffer's writings and also Bethge's great biography of him while an undergraduate in Oxford was certainly one of the factors that led to my decision to become a priest in the Church of England. It was Peter Walker, however, who urged me to delve more deeply into Bonhoeffer's story and to weigh all the difficult issues that he and others confronted during such terrible times. Peter emphasized the courageous realism that colours all of Bonhoeffer's theology as he wrestled with how the gospel could engage modern society, as well as challenge a cruel and destructive dictatorship. Bonhoeffer's challenge to the rest of the Lutheran Church was no less stern, as he openly resisted apostasy and any compromise with an unscrupulous and racist regime.

Bonhoeffer's home and upbringing in Berlin was a professional and affluent one, and his family were surprised when he decided to read theology and become a Lutheran pastor. But they were a close-knit family group, who in the end paid a high price for their resistance to Hitler. Bonhoeffer grew up in the turbulence of Berlin after the end of the First World War with its violence and political frustration, and the bitter experience of hyper-inflation not once but twice within a decade. He spotted early on the implications of antisemitism for German society and also for the life and integrity of the Protestant Church, and he called it out for what it was. In 1934 he supported the Barmen Declaration by which the Confessing Church repudiated the Nazi domination of the state Church, causing a painful schism. For his own safety, Bonhoeffer was sent to England, and he used his time well in getting to know the life of the Church of England. His friendship with Bishop George Bell as an older and more experienced priest was of decisive importance and encouragement to him to the end of his days.

When he chose to return from America at the outbreak of war in 1939, Bonhoeffer was able to use his ecumenical and other contacts to keep in touch with Bell, and to apprise him of the hopes of those opposed to Hitler's regime. Bell communicated these to the British government, which did not give them any credibility or encouragement. In the end, Bonhoeffer faced the agonizing decision of how far to go in plotting the downfall of the regime in the midst of a terrible war. He came to the hard decision as a Christian that the murder of Hitler would be justified because it was necessary to stop the madness. The plot failed in the summer of

1944, disastrously for all involved, and Bonhoeffer was arrested and executed along with other conspirators: he was hanged on 9 April 1945, just before the war ended.

I have always found Bonhoeffer's story and his writings deeply moving, and they convinced me that Christianity is of decisive importance in sustaining a free and democratic society under the rule of law. This remains the single most important issue today—in every part of the world. Bonhoeffer's memory convinced me also that a Christian priest has to be fearless in teaching and upholding the principles that spring from the gospel, and that these alone can provide a sure basis for human life everywhere. This conviction led me to see the role of a teaching chaplain among so many young people for so many years as a most worthwhile way to be a priest. To enable properly informed choices and to cultivate genuine compassion seem to be the essential tasks of any Christian teacher among young people, appealing to their own sense of justice and compassion, while equipping them with an intelligent grasp of the gospel. Teaching about the choices of Bonhoeffer and others like him when confronting dictatorship, and indicating the causes of prejudice, discrimination and violence shed a sharp light on the relevance of the gospel in any society. Young people deserve to be given the opportunity to think about these things and then to make their own free and informed choices.

Dietrich Bonhoeffer was a Lutheran pastor, and fortunately circumstances enabled me to make friends with Lutherans in Austria and also in Latvia. We exchanged with a Protestant family in Austria as teenagers, one of whom became a pastor in the church there, which is a hybrid Lutheran–Calvinist entity created as one of the conditions for its toleration at the end of the eighteenth century. At the time of Elizabeth I, Austria was more Protestant than England; but this was crushed by the Hapsburg monarchy with the collusion of the Catholic Church. When I first got to know the family, memories of persecution and antipathy towards the Catholic Church were still strong among some in the Protestant Church there. They had been as a family opposed to Hitler, and the older generation had served in the war in grim conditions as it ended, and when Lower Austria was occupied by the Russians until 1955.

This experience of encountering a minority Church that had endured repeated persecution and hardship equipped me for visits to Latvia many years later, where I formed a strong friendship with the new young Archbishop of Riga and one of his energetic younger pastors. There had been a strong British trading relationship with Riga before the Second World War that stretched back into the nineteenth century. The former Anglican church was still being used as a cinema, though it has since been returned to the Anglican chaplaincy there. One of the purposes of my visits was to rekindle this relationship in various practical ways as well as by personal friendships. The quiet dignity of Lutheran worship made a great impression on me along with its profound musical tradition, which was very strong in Latvia. I felt at the time that I was following the example of Bishop George Bell and finding myself greatly enriched by my many encounters with Christians there, Orthodox and Old Believers as well as Lutherans and Catholics.

Peter Walker also had a great love of poetry and a real affinity with some modern Christians poets like T. S. Eliot, R. S. Thomas, and especially with the poetry of Geoffrey Hill. The root of this sensibility lay deep for him in the poetry of George Herbert, and he used often to quote from Herbert's lovely poem about the nature of Prayer:

> Prayer the church's banquet, angel's age,
> God's breath in man returning to his birth,
> The soul in paraphrase, heart in pilgrimage,
> The Christian plummet sounding heav'n and earth
> Engine against th' Almighty, sinner's tow'r,
> Reversed thunder, Christ-side-piercing spear,
> The six-days world transposing in an hour,
> A kind of tune, which all things hear and fear;
> Softness, and peace, and joy, and love, and bliss,
> Exalted manna, gladness of the best,
> Heaven in ordinary, man well drest,
> The milky way, the bird of Paradise,
> Church-bells beyond the stars
>     heard, the soul's blood,
> The land of spices; something understood.

Peter felt keenly that language is only ever the tip of the reality it attempts to express, and that it should never be forced. The words of Scripture have to be approached with careful poetic sensitivity for this very reason.

Peter's love of St Augustine came from the fact that he too was a deeply sensitive person with a poetic mastery of language and a keen aesthetic sensibility. It was not therefore appropriate to receive what he wrote simply in a didactic way, but rather to listen for its hidden depths. When Peter preached, this poetic yearning for words that could convey true meaning was very apparent—hence the long pauses for thought and expression. As a Christian priest he always pointed beyond himself, and his use of language to this end was profoundly moving, memorable and formative. A preacher can never know what depths he or she will touch in a human heart: there has to be a silent dialogue of love with those listening, which springs from a loving dialogue with God Himself. Dogmatism has no place in the pulpit or in the classroom, nor in pastoral conversations either.

Peter Walker set an abiding example of how to listen to people and to respond to their deepest needs, patiently and sensitively, but also with a firm wisdom: he was a model of friendship and a true friend. His perception of others and empathy sprang from his honest and humble perception of himself, well expressed in these words of George Herbert:

> Lord, Thou art mine, and I am mine,
> if mine I am: and Thine much more,
> than I or ought, or can be mine;
> yet to be Thine, doth me restore.

Friendship restored with God is at the heart of the gospel, and therefore Christian friendship with others is, as Alcuin taught, participation within the love of God.

8

# Mary Clare

*Seeking the saints*

I first got to know Mother Mary Clare as I was finishing my first degree in Modern History and preparing to read Theology as an ordinand at Cuddesdon. She came to speak about the nature of prayer in the first Michaelmas term and invited me to visit her in her retirement at the convent of the Sisters of the Love of God at Fairacres in Oxford. We struck up an immediate rapport and she was a great support to me when dealing with some of the difficult moments in ordination training. She also proved to be a firm friend to my wife, and she offered us every encouragement in the early years of our married life, as well as in our own vocations. During her time as Mother, she had opened up the community from being a strictly enclosed life to developing a ministry of embracing visitors and friends, near and far, that enabled them to enter within its hidden life of contemplative prayer and intercession.

She wrote clearly and well about the Christian vocation to "contemplative intercession", as she called it, to which she believed that priests are also called alongside those committed by their vows to the contemplative life. Mother Mary Clare was gently formidable, demanding, but always loving, and she blessed and guided many lives. She conveyed a real sense that the contemplative path is open to any Christian who sincerely seeks it; and that to be "in stillness nailed, to hold all time, all change, all circumstance, to and in Love's embrace" is the heart of prayer, both within the heart, and also at the altar of the Eucharist. She also made very accessible the essential teaching of St Teresa of Ávila and St John of the Cross, and his poems have been a constant companion to my own prayers ever since. I have also found the theological writings of Hans Urs von Balthasar to be a sure guide to the contemplative life of prayer.

Contemplative intercession is at the heart of being a priest, bearing people in the heart, and standing alongside Christ himself in his hour of grieving and compassion for them. It also means engaging with and enduring some of the world's darkness and pain. Regular annual retreats, for many years mostly at Fairacres, have been a vital foundation for being a priest; and my path into contemplative prayer has been a true pilgrimage of grace, closely associated with holy places and holy writings, and certainly nurtured by them. As a child, I grew up familiar with St Albans Abbey and Canterbury Cathedral, and later with St David's Cathedral as well. Each of these places left an indelible mark on my imagination and sense of the reality of God, and also of the rich continuity of Christian history in our country. The ruined church at Reculver on the north coast of Kent, where an early Anglo-Saxon monastery was created within the walls of a deserted Roman fort, made a vivid and lasting impression on my memory and imagination even as a very young child. What was a monastery, I wondered, and why were they destroyed? Visits to the Community of the Resurrection at Mirfield as an undergraduate, where a friend was training for the priesthood, gave me my first experience of a monastic community, which was further cultivated by our strong friendships with the Sisters of the Love of God in Oxford, and later with the Community of St Mary the Virgin at Wantage. We have also greatly benefited from a strong friendship with the Benedictine community of Douai Abbey in Berkshire. The stability of Benedictine life and prayer has underpinned the whole development of the *Ecclesia Anglicana*.

Holidays with our children near Lindisfarne and the Farne Islands, coupled with regular visits to Durham while two of them were students there, further deepened this sense of the living past of Christianity in England. The conjunction of reading about and visiting such places has proved to be a way in which various saints have become real as persons: Dunstan and Anselm at Canterbury; Mildred of Minster-in-Thanet and Etheldreda at Ely; Aidan, Cuthbert and Bede in the northeast of England. Wales too has always exerted a subtle spiritual influence, as Christianity is so deeply rooted there: the beauty and remoteness of places like St David's, Bardsey Island and Pennant Melangell radiate a sense of the hidden reality of God. One saint of Anglesey in particular, St Seiriol, who lived at Penmon where his cell can still be seen, epitomized and made real to me the hidden witness of prayer from that very early period of Christian life in Wales.

Visits in Europe have often made a comparable impact: for example, at the tomb of St Willibrord at Echternach, who went to the Continent from England as a missionary in the eighth century. But it is our many visits to Rome and more generally in Italy that have conveyed most strongly the full meaning of the communion of saints—*communio sanctorum*—of people, places and books, all gathered together within the worship of the Eucharist as the eternal act of communion that unites all Christians everywhere and across the ages. My first evening in Rome as a schoolboy in 1968 was spent in St Peter's Basilica for the Easter Vigil and Blessing of the New Fire being led by Pope Paul VI himself, who remains in my mind's eye as he processed down the nave, a slight and gracious figure. The ancient churches that surround San Gregorio al Celio, where we often stayed as friends of the Camaldolese Benedictines, convey the deep truth that the Roman Church was founded upon martyrdom. Among all the lovely early churches of the Eternal City, it is the noble basilica of St Paul-outside-the-Walls that draws my heart, and this is always the first port of call on any visit to Rome. It is where the apostle is buried is a church of awesome beauty and dignity; to kneel there is to be at the threshold of the apostles—*ad limina apostolorum*.

The whole Church owes a great debt to the saints of Italy: for the English in particular, St Gregory the Great has always been "the apostle" who sent St Augustine as a missionary to Kent in 597. St Anselm, one of the greatest Archbishops of Canterbury, also came from northern Italy. To stay at San Gregorio al Celio is to sense the reality of this rich legacy; and to make a retreat at Camaldoli up in the mountains and forests of the Casentino is to draw near to St Romuald and his contemplative monastic vision of a thousand years ago. To visit Assisi is to draw close in particular to St Clare, whose church and body made such a deep impression on our children. To visit La Verna is to kneel on the rocky place where St Francis received the stigmata and to sense his profound holiness. To visit Bagnoregio near Orvieto is to see what remains of the hometown of St Bonaventure. Each of these saints has become real as a person, set in a particular place and time "where prayer has been valid". It has been a great privilege to have been able to study their lives and to be moulded by their teaching and prayers.

We have always had a strong friendship with Orthodox Christians throughout our marriage and have been blessed by worshipping with friends in the Orthodox churches in Oxford and Bath, and by the friendship and encouragement of the late Archbishop Antony Bloom. As Communism was coming to an end in the Soviet Union, we were able to visit Russia and Ukraine, and also the Baltic states of Latvia and Lithuania. It was a time of hope and of creating new relationships between Christians, often for the first time. The writings of St Nilus and St Theophan the Recluse have had a decisive and lasting influence on my own life of prayer. A visit to the shrine of St Sergius, and a moving encounter with the newly recovered relics of St Seraphim of Sarov, at Easter 1991 in Moscow, conveyed the reality of these two saints in deep and unforgettable ways. No less important were more hidden visits to a Poustinka in the forests near Riga in Latvia associated with a priest called Father Tavrion, who had survived many harsh years of suffering in the Gulag. To encounter the costly witness of countless Russian Christians and others in the face of atheism and cruelty was astonishing and deeply moving. It was also shattering to witness the ravages of antisemitism in those troubled lands and to make strong friendships with some Jewish families and academics still living there.

No less formative was a pilgrimage we made in 2008 with The Friends of Mount Athos to the ancient monastery of St Catherine's below Mount Sinai. This included walking out to the site of the earliest hermitages, and also to the cell of St John Climacus in a cave in a remote wadi in the desert nearby. It was crowned by a long private conversation with a hermit in a cave above the monastery, and by a night-time ascent to the summit of Sinai to witness the dawn as it spread across the red granite mountain tops. During the day there was a great abundance of light and a keen sense that this was the place where God's dialogue of self-revelation with human beings began with Moses and still continues. This was particularly true during the Divine Liturgy in the ancient basilica built by Justinian with its wonderful apse mosaic of the Transfiguration. The brilliance of the whole place and its silence conveyed the vigour of the resurrection and of eternal day, and at night the nearness and beauty of the stars was overwhelming.

This pilgrimage then took us to the austere desert monasteries of St Antony and of St Paul by the Red Sea, and concluded with visits to four monasteries in the Wadi Natrun, where regular monastic life in the desert began and has recently been restored. The renewal of monastic life in Egypt that we encountered during these visits gave added force and immediacy to the witness of St Mary of Egypt and the wisdom and teaching of the Desert Fathers and Mothers. The modern witness and writings of Matthew the Poor are within this tradition: he lived at the monastery of St Macarius in the Wadi Natrun and for 30 years was its spiritual father.

It was Pope St John Paul II who said that the Church must breathe with its two lungs—Eastern and Western, and it has been a privilege to be able to experience something of what this means in terms of such wide and varied ecumenical exchanges and friendships. The Orthodox monastery in Essex, founded by St Sophrony, has proved to be a true spiritual home. Its warmth of community life and creativity is matched by unfailing hospitality and devout worship that centres around the use of the Jesus Prayer, privately in the cell and publicly in divine worship, normally in the evening at Vespers when it is quietly recited aloud in various languages. This ancient and simple prayer is the anchor of Orthodox monastic life: "Lord Jesus Christ, Son of the Living God, have mercy on me a sinner." The monastery keeps alive the memory and teaching of St Silouan the Athonite, who lived at the Russian monastery of St Panteleimon and whom St Sophrony got to know while living there before the Second World War. Sophrony's vocation was to make the witness and teaching of this hidden Russian saint known and to write his *Life*, which is one of the finest hagiographies of recent times. St Silouan was commanded by God to keep his mind in hell and never to despair, as by his prayers he engaged the darkness enveloping Europe and his own homeland, Russia. It was through the good offices of the Abbot of the Essex monastery and also of the late Bishop Kallistos Ware that I was enabled to visit the Holy Mountain of Athos, where I subsequently made many annual pilgrimages to the monasteries of Vatopedi and Simonospetra, normally in Lent.

The renewal of monastic life on Mount Athos is one of the miracles of our own lifetime, and to visit there is to encounter a living tradition of worship and prayer that creates saints such as St Paisios, St Porphyrios and St Joseph the Hesychast. The tomb of St Joseph at the New Skete is a place of simplicity and quiet, but it was his indefatigable life of ascetic prayer with others that laid the foundation for the renewal of regular monastic life that has since occurred on Athos and elsewhere, including in America. The cave of St Symeon, who founded the monastery of Simonospetra in the Middle Ages, is another holy place of quietness, punctuated only by the gushing of water in the spring within the rock hard by. Most memorable perhaps is the skete of Kavsokalivia on the very tip of the peninsula and virtually under the mountain of Athos itself as it plunges into the sea. This is a place so quiet that its holiness is palpable and the sense of God the Trinity is very near during the starlit night. The desert of Athos is still the habitation of hermits, whose homes can be seen from the boat, perched along the precipitous cliffs of Kerasia and Karoulia.

These visits, spread over more than a decade, proved to be a true school of prayer. Once again books interpreted places and places provide their context: the writings of St Symeon the New Theologian, St Gregory of Sinai and St Gregory Palamas come to life when set within this remarkable and hidden environment of ascetic life and prayer. Central to this whole tradition is *The Philokalia*, now available in an English translation in five volumes. There is no surer or more comprehensive guide to the spiritual life and the use of the Jesus Prayer in contemplative intercession. Apart from the Bible, no other book has made such a continuous and formative impression through many years on my own understanding of spiritual reality and the dynamic of prayer itself.

To pray is to be transformed and to stand on the threshold of eternity, embracing and being embraced by the great silence of Divine Love. Seeking this encounter and bowing before it is the goal of all Christian contemplation: it is to stand in the presence of the Risen Christ himself. But at the same time, such humble contemplation is drawn into deep intercession for the world's needs. The use of the Jesus Prayer also encourages comparable prayer to the Holy Mother of God, the Blessed Virgin Mary, for the life of the Church and the world. For it is her compassionate intercession and friendship that sustains the life of the Church and its saints and nurtures the aspirations of every loving soul.

The Communion of Saints is therefore the matrix within which Christian life grows and thrives. It is deeply relational in character, as persons past and present, who are indwelt by the Holy Spirit, are drawn together into a loving communion of worship, contemplation and intercession. It comprises the fascinating interaction of holy people, holy places and holy writings across time and space. It is a privilege today to be able to access such a rich treasury of spiritual writings, often available in translation, that are drawn from across the whole Church, Eastern and Western, and to be free and able to visit so many holy places and to make friends there. Herein lies the hidden unity of the Church as something real and wonderful: for Christianity is essentially a loving communion of friends, whose life is rooted in Christ, and who share the same gift of the indwelling Holy Spirit.

# Conclusion

*Contemplative intercession*

I have drawn together some reflections from a private spiritual journal written during retreats with the Sisters of the Love of God at Fairacres in Oxford, to try to convey the meaning of contemplative intercession; these are set in chronological order as my own life and vocation as a priest unfolded. I have used the format often found in *The Philokalia*, where thought is often distilled into succinct paragraphs, and which are sometimes numbered as well. The closing series of reflections arose during many retreats on the Holy Mountain of Athos at the monasteries of Vatopedi and Simonospetra, or among the Carthusians.

### At Fairacres

1. Our relationship with God must bear the impress of His character: Silence, Simplicity, and Love.

2. As a wick floats in a lamp of oil and so gives light to a worshipper, so a priest becomes an intermediary for the Holy Spirit: everything—yet nothing in himself or herself.
3. Adversity in the Christian spiritual life is like grit in an oyster: no grit, no pearl.
4. Prayer burnishes the soul, and character is etched deeper by suffering borne in love.
5. At the Eucharist, a priest must bear something of the pain of Christ's betrayal, so that the life-giving power of God may flow out to meet the needs of His people. Such ministry is "sacrificial because joyful and joyful because sacrificial" (Michael Ramsey).
6. There are three hallmarks of a saint: spiritual vision, prayerful patience, and joyful love. A saint is someone who makes God real and near, being full of joy.
7. In a new-born baby may be glimpsed the unsullied glory of a human person made in the image of God, and in a tiny child's vulnerability and complete dependence lies a clue to the human likeness and affinity to God as He comes to us in the person of Jesus.
8. Within the dynamic of faith, suffering and love, a person discovers common ground with God, as this is at the heart of Calvary.

9. A child once said, "Heaven is simple really: it is very large, because it is where God is; but the way into it is very small because it is in our hearts."
10. Contemplation and intercession are the inward and the outward breathing of the Holy Spirit within a human heart and mind: they constitute two facets of worship.
11. There should be three hallmarks of a Christian response to someone: discernment, dialogue, and devotion. If in doubt, always be kind.
12. Do not recoil from Christ's *Via Crucis*, because that which is not of God's will is nonetheless never outside His will: for the hands in which He sustains the world are wounded in love.
13. As a person feels towards their own children, so the Lord feels towards everyone. Using this natural impulse and affection as a spur and guide, we must allow the Spirit to expand our love towards others until we begin to sense the way in which God feels towards them. Then our love is caught up within His, and our love for them becomes a sure channel for, and an expression of, His great and indestructible love for them.
14. Hope moves through love to express itself in patience, and trust meets its supreme test in forgiveness: this is the depth, extent, cost and strength of Christ-like love—to become able "to put his love in where love is not" (St John of the Cross).

15. Contemplative prayer comprises simplicity, detachment and love unbounded: it is "the one thing needful" at the heart of everything, and to this goal every gift and energy should be directed.
16. True gentleness is in fact moral strength that is divinely controlled and transformed; for "Thy gentleness has made me strong." "To the Lord belong judgement and mercy", which are the two faces of divine Love; but to human beings belongs only the exercise of mercy.
17. Charity and discrimination balance each other, as charity without discrimination lapses into blinkered sentimentality; discrimination untempered by charity quickly becomes hypercritical of others. Only if the Holy Spirit is Lord of all our relationships and thinking can this crucial balance be sustained.
18. In the ministry of contemplative intercession, we must join our prayers with those of the Holy Mother of the Lord and implore her prayers and aid for us first: for it is she who leads the saints in the great outreach of sacrificial and healing love that flows from the heart of God.
19. The proclamation of Mary—the *Magnificat*—and also those of the saints proclaim the eternal destiny of human beings: hence the profound spiritual opposition whenever this occurs, lest the true call of God to men and women should be heard, or the heavenly vision be indelibly glimpsed.

20. Blindness to the reality and activity of the saints in their constant prayer and compassionate outreach effectively paralyses the spiritual life of a church.
21. Each inkling of the heavenly existence of redeemed humanity induces an acute sense of joyful and tearful tenderness, and this is particularly so when the Virgin Mother herself draws near. Her gracious and loving humility begins to transform everything.
22. A hallmark of sanctity is a radical and childlike simplicity, which is a mingling of sensitivity and strength, being a true expression of joyful love and trust in all their human tenderness.
23. At the giving of communion, a priest joins himself or herself to the complete self-giving of Christ to each communicant. In that quiet and private moment, the ceaselessness of the divine movement of outpouring love may be sensed, and also the heavenly reality of the Body of Christ.
24. We may conceive of heaven in its relationship with earthly life as an endless movement more deeply into divine Love, a fountain of rehabilitation in which divine Love reaches out to human beings *through* other human beings, and supremely through the humanity of Christ, both in this world and the next.
25. All human choices are part of an ineluctable pattern: Love or unlove? That is all, and that is

the key to the whole meaning of life. Essentially, on which side of the Cross do you stand?

26. A priest has to be schooled in humiliation in order better to assist in God's work of unravelling the tragedy of human pride.

27. The effects of pride in others are these: anger, demoralization, fear, and a sense of dread about the future. The antidote lies in reaching out in faith, hope and love—to each other first, and then, if possible, to the victims of pride, for arrogance is always a sign of weakness and a delusion.

28. To be within the will of God is to become a "plough" in the Lord's hands, whereby He breaks open the hard surface of this world, and so enables the new life of the Kingdom to spring up—but long *after* the plough has passed on. Christ does not look back and nor must we, even if we feel nose down in the dirt, assailed and under pressure on all sides, being relentlessly opposed: for we are in His hands after all.

29. An angel conveys grace from on high in an immediate and effective way to rescue and heal us in our hour of desperate need. Then we perceive that our skirmishes are but the outskirts of a wider and higher conflict, whose parameters can scarcely be apprehended.

30. Growth in Christlikeness means responding to the leading of the Holy Spirit "into all truth". The key to this lies in His "speaking the truth in

love" to us, and our "speaking the truth in love" to each other. Thus listening, learning and loving constitute a dynamic pattern of movement of the heart and mind into God, which also draws us closer to others in Him. So, in listening let us learn; and in learning let us love; in loving let us live, now, and in eternity.

31. Intercession spans the distance between praying for those whom we naturally love the most, and praying by the grace of the Holy Spirit for those whom God calls us at any one time to love the most, or who need to be loved the most, even if this is against the grain of our natural inclinations.

32. Under spiritual assault we should cling to God, as each hammering chips away a small part of the hardened mantle of original sin: our hubris must be smashed daily on the rock at the foot of the Cross.

33. Self-forgetfulness in the worship of God and in service to others is the road towards true and genuine contemplative humility. Our duty is to be vigilant towards all the many subtle ways in which we are *not* being humble, for true Christian prayer is always humble contemplation in the midst of conflict, while engaging the world's darkness.

34. The "Jesus Prayer" is the eternal prayer of the saints, and it is also a prayer *with* the saints in the Holy Spirit, who breathes within us and lets God love Himself through us (*amet se teipso*—"let God

love Himself through you"—St Augustine): for the perplexity and pain caused within us is that of life returning, eroding the numbness of our souls.

35. On God's side, there has never been any failure to love, and the Cross demonstrates this, putting all failures of human love into a true perspective; this is the judgement of divine Love.

36. The work of the Holy Spirit in Church history reverses the normal human experience of "change and decay" into "decay and change", as Christians pass through death to life, by "living through dying", and the visible Church is gradually conformed to its true and heavenly archetype.

37. A saint's life vindicates every line of the psalms, revealing the nature of a lifetime of profoundly Christ-centred love: it becomes a re-enactment of the gospel, and it is this that determines the character of the best Christian hagiography.

38. Moment by moment, our choice at the heart of prayer is a very simple one: pride, or Jesus himself? The "Jesus Prayer" and the Lord's Prayer are our most effective weapons against the insinuations of evil and pride, as is the ancient Benedictine invocation used in the divine office: "O God, make speed to save us: O Lord, make haste to help us."

39. The Eucharist is the fountain of unceasing divine Love, which flows at supreme cost from the heart of the crucified Christ for the life of the Church

and the healing of the world, and it flows through us every time we celebrate or receive Holy Communion.

40. Every angle of a saint's life, teaching and character points to the one source of its manifold expression, for a saint becomes a unique embodiment of the Holy Spirit, who dwells within a person, making all things new, and so fulfilling and perfecting the divine image and likeness in someone who truly loves Him.

41. In every generation, God raises up light-bearers and life-givers within the life of the Church, who act like repeater stations transmitting the light of the Resurrection; and this is part of the spiritual meaning of the Apostolic Succession.

42. At the Eucharist, a priest may pass from standing on earth at the threshold of heaven to standing within heaven itself: then the priest as the mediator of divine Love faces the earth in a totally different way. Signs of this are a certain kind of light, fire in the chalice, the charism of tears, and a profound and joyful sense of peace, supported by the presence of angels, that becomes the wellspring of serene vision and boundless love, all enfolded within the immense silence of God's own presence.

43. "To enter with Christ into heaven itself and also into the world's darkness: that is the meaning of Calvary" (Michael Ramsey). Christian

reconciliation within the life of the Church can only be attained in a spirit of penitential awe, reverence, humility and silence. For a saint's worship and vision is rooted in the silence and the immensity of God Himself—in the nearness of His reality and being held within His love.

44. The charism of true Christian authority should enable others to live and flourish; it should point them from simply being or existing towards their true wellbeing in Christ, and then towards their vocation to share in eternal being: a deeply spiritual person deepens personality in others, often liberating human relationships too.

45. Nature is the handmaid of prayer, and silent repose within it restores the soul: the essential nature of our relationship with God is a profound and complete simplicity and rest within the immense reality of His presence, which nature often mediates to us by its peace, perfection and beauty.

46. Before we can put love in where love is not, we must first let love in to us where love is not, and then the Holy Spirit will leave no door within the heart unopened.

47. Unsought suffering inflicted by evil is actually not futile, even if it feels so, for by the grace of the Holy Spirit within us it may be freely offered up as costly intercession for that which is its cause. Perhaps this is one of the ways in which the grace

and love of God actually transform human nature, in us, and also in others; for human spiritual solidarity and sensitivity are far more profound that we realize or allow for, as we are all one in the Body of Christ.

48. Intercession for the chronically captive is a tortuous and afflicted path, usually assailed by disappointment, and its end is often unknown to us. It entails wrestling with the evil that emanates, while at the same time praying faithfully for the human person who is blinded and enslaved. The person becomes the object of love, while evil lies at the root of the conflict, and we feel its soul-destroying tendency, its implications, and its pain.

49. The result of spiritual conflict is always to throw a person more simply, directly and deeply into the love of God as into a vast ocean.

50. Contemplative intercession is both a chalice and a well: it is a chalice of suffering to be drained to the bitter dregs, but it is also a well of life and light, as the Holy Spirit is drawn up within us, in order to flow out, and be breathed out in life-giving love and prayer for the Church and the world. This sharp contrast springs directly from Calvary, and it is perhaps part of the meaning of our Lord's promise that "out of the heart will flow rivers of living water", as well as the evangelist's recognition of the significance of water and blood flowing from the pierced heart of Christ on the Cross.

51. The greater the light, the deeper the darkness: the nearer the glory, the sharper the pain. But in the end, eternal life is simply a more deeply and truly human life, rooted directly in God, and permeated by His Spirit of Love, a life that transcends time and space.
52. As we are drawn more deeply into the mystery of the Cross, so we learn to pray with Christ on his Cross and in his own words in order to fulfil his own commandment to us to love one another, and also to love our enemies. Through this costly intercession, Christ's life and love and healing flow out through our own life that is now hidden with him in God.
53. Calvary means humiliation, compassion and intercession, and how we share in Christ's sufferings is perhaps a decisive bond of love and empathy between us and Christ himself.
54. Prayer is therefore not so much what we owe to Christ, but what he wills to accomplish in and through us. We have to pray diligently, however, to sustain the life of Christ within us, which is now our own life in him, our embracing him in love.
55. When in the quiet of prayer, the mind descends deep into the heart, a person becomes reconciled and united within. The inner silence, at once immense and tender, is the communion of a person with God by the indwelling of the Holy

Spirit. This is the promised "well of living water springing up to eternal life".

56. In prayer we simply place ourselves, small as we are, within the great beam of divine light, life and love, which streams forth from the Lord's countenance and presence. Thus we are found in Him; and if others spring forth in our heart and memory at that time, they too are found in Him, as we carry them in our heart and memory.

57. A Christian miracle is the healing of the whole personality by God, often in unexpected ways, and sometimes through other people, but always in a way that is deeply personal, compassionate, healing and reconciling.

58. All the world's evil and all inhumanity sear the Body of Christ on Calvary, for we are indeed members one of another. But how his vicarious suffering is redemptive is mostly beyond our ken. Yet deification begins here at the "still turning-point" of time and eternity, where life and love are reborn out of suffering and sorrow, and vision is forever changed. For at Calvary, two darknesses collide: the world's desolation and the vastness of God and His love.

59. "To bide His time and see His glory" (Peter Walker). These words capture one of the consequences of prayer by our humble exposure to God, beginning to see things from a divine rather than a human perspective. Such purposeful

patience is a hallmark of divine Love working within us, altering our attitudes and values.

60. Prayer is not doing—it is simply *being*, often in a place of complete powerlessness: no longer praying for anything, but simply praying in the Lord's presence, and therein lies its power.

61. In moments of private prayer, we must seek with divine help the opening of our hearts in complete tenderness: to such tenderness the Holy Spirit cannot fail to respond, as the Spirit enables it and participates in it.

62. We are called to perpetual intercession by day and night with our eyes fixed on Jesus: we are each called to become a fountain of divine Love for the Church and for the world.

63. We should pray as if we are responsible to some extent for every circumstance of which we are aware or in which we are involved, for in the place of prayer we are indeed responsible for one another, and our prayers can reach where we cannot be (St Gregory the Great).

64. Contemplative intercession consists of self-emptying, or *kenosis*, and complete self-forgetfulness in the presence of God: it means openness of heart and love towards Him in order to become channels of His compassion to others, known and unknown. For our soul is like a mirror that must be burnished and cherished each day by our prayer.

65. Our life must become like an empty chalice set before God: precious, single of purpose, clean, stable and open to him. Then the fire of the Spirit will descend within us, as it does in the chalice of the Eucharist itself.
66. The Church exists to mediate the reality of the resurrection, and the work of divine grace is to restore the natural to normal, to bring about "perfection in the midst of imperfection" (St Gregory the Great), and then to transform it for ever in glory.

## On the Holy Mountain

67. The place for contemplative intercession is kneeling or prostrate on the rock at the foot of the Cross, hard by the empty tomb, and then passing quietly through the open door, which leads to the vista of the divine abyss of God's being and also the vision of the darkness of His love; this is the secret place where the angels sing "*Hagios! Hagios! Hagios!*"—"Holy! Holy! Holy!" across the great deep.
68. The mystery of the holy Mother with her child Jesus is a profound one: her desire is that we should love and cherish her Son as our friend. The horror of his rejection, torture and crucifixion hovers in

the wings of this vision, as a dark shadow of pain for him and also for her as his mother.

69. When Jesus spoke about receiving the Kingdom of God as a child, he spoke not only of our own attitude towards God as our Father and towards all children, but also of receiving the Kingdom in his own person as a child or young person. The youthfulness of the holy Mother of God is also palpable and striking, and it is important to recognize and cherish both Mother and Son. In the presence of God the Father, holding the holy Mother and her child in His Love, all is simply silence and love—and a bright darkness.

70. The great vista of the Holy Mountain itself was transfigured and transfiguring by the sun's light streaming over its snowy peak. It felt a glimpse of a new heaven and a new earth, because transfiguration and resurrection are two facets of the same divine reality. This *transitus*, however brief, from death to life, from shadow to reality, and into such love and light gives new depth to the meaning and beauty of the words of the Scriptures and of the liturgy: it is like being *within* them.

71. During divine worship in the two monasteries, which is all in Greek, the tongue of the heart remains silent though still expressive, as its prayer underlies all the words of prayer and liturgy in whatever language. The music of the chanting

echoes in the soul as an outpouring of silence and love: its source and exemplar are angelic.

72. The Holy Mountain, like Sinai and Camaldoli, feels like "home" because it is part of the heavenly Mountain of the Lord. Its hidden reality may also be sensed within the microcosm of the heart, with all its heights and hidden ways in which Christ's presence within us may be encountered.

73. Tears of compunction and joy are signs of our unity with the deep empathy of Christ himself, for contemplation and intercession are two sides of his loving compassion and therefore of ours.

74. Christ veils his presence deliberately to enable our relationship with him to develop in a natural and authentic way: it is an act of purposeful self-restraint that is marked by love and respect for those whom he calls to become his friends. The manner of the Incarnation is the supreme expression of this divine self-restraint and humility.

75. Our words fail before the Word, from whom nonetheless they spring; only silence and tears remain, along with a hushed sensitivity to the Beauty that descends.

76. Byzantine music seems to plumb and delineate the hidden depths and ways of the human heart at prayer, for these are the Lord's ways that we must follow by love and prayer, thus entering into the

divine Silence and Beauty that eclipses all human words.
77. Silence, worship and love spring from compunction, contrition and humility.
78. We are called to be *within* the Silence that descends; to worship is simply to be and to offer, not just to do or to say.
79. Deep within a person, behind the altar of the heart, is the locked ark in which the soul is protected by the angels until the day when divine grace elects to open its door as a skilled and patient physician. The door of Paradise was slammed shut and guarded partly for the protection of the soul that is made in the image and likeness of God, with its profound affinity to the very Being of God Himself. Then the soul, which is simple, ancient and primordial, emerges as a child with its own voice of praise and beauty: this mystery is portrayed in the Orthodox icon of the Dormition.
80. Mind and heart are doorkeepers to the inner sanctuary of the Lord, which is the altar of the heart, for "heaven is the country of the soul" (St Augustine).
81. The intention of God the Father is to restore human beings to friendship with Himself through the person of Jesus and with the support of his holy Mother. God's yearning compassion is expressed by His love outpoured in Christ, and revealed by the evident pain of His frustration at human

wills that are trapped in their insensitivity and perversity, for only the human will can withstand God if it so chooses. The work of our Lord and his holy Mother is to make the Father known and truly loved by *koinonia* or communion in the Holy Spirit, who seeks to enfold us all within the Father's love.

82. Why is so precious an entity as the soul embodied in so turbulent, vulnerable and fragile a human person? It is surely "to put Love in where love is not" and to enable the human person willingly to become by that Love the sanctuary of the indwelling Holy Spirit.

83. Damage to the soul is therefore an unbearable thought and tragedy, and a torment to it. The broken heart of the holy Mother of God, in all its bitter trauma, is terrible to sense, but it is the wellspring of her compassion, her bond with us, ever seeking to remake human beings in love and to safeguard their souls.

84. The priest celebrating is called to be clothed in the divine Silence and to be within the prayer of the Holy Spirit. For it is the Spirit that unites our prayer and worship with the inspired and sacramental language of liturgy and Scripture in all its manifold depth and mystery.

85. Relics of saints are sacramental instruments used by the Holy Spirit to heal and convert the

soul: they participate tangibly in that which they signify, and they mediate its blessing and healing.

86. Tenderness is fundamental to intercession and prayer to Christ, or to his holy Mother, for tenderness is the loving expression of humility and sobriety, also called *nepsis*.

87. The unity between the soul and a person is sealed by the Holy Spirit, and the consecration of all desire enables the prayer of the soul, which should be cared for as a little child.

88. The soul seeks union with the incarnate Christ by means of the consecration of the desires of the flesh, as well as of the mind and the heart: then *cor ad cor loquitur*—heart speaks to heart (St John Henry Newman).

89. We are called to be found *in sinu Filii Dei* just as he is the *Unigenitus Dei Filius qui est in sinu Patris* (John 1:18): that is, to be found within the heart of Christ, as he is within the Father's heart, and to be made like him by being enfolded within the Love of the Holy Trinity.

90. For God's love within us is indeed an abyss, whose depths cannot be sounded: and in His will is our peace.

## A prayer of St Thérèse of Lisieux

O my God, you know that I have never
 wanted anything but to love You alone.
Your Love opened up before me in my
 childhood and in my first love.
It has grown within me, and now it is an
 abyss, whose depths I cannot sound.

# Further reading

Aimilianos, Archimandrite, *The Way of the Spirit* (Athens: Indiktos Press, 2009).

Allchin, A. M., *The World is a Wedding: Exploration in Christian Spirituality* (London: Darton, Longman & Todd, 1978).

Allchin, A. M., *Participation in God: A Forgotten Strand in Anglican Tradition* (London: Darton, Longman & Todd, 1988).

Allchin, A. M., *The Joy of All Creation: An Anglican Meditation on the Place of Mary* (London: New City, 1993).

Allchin, A. M., *The Gift of Theology: The Trinitarian Vision of Ann Griffiths and Elizabeth of Dijon* [i.e. Elizabeth of the Trinity] (Oxford: SLG Press, 2005).

Allchin, A. M. (ed.), *Solitude and Communion: Papers on the Hermit Life* (Oxford: SLG Press, 2014).

Balthasar, H. Urs von., *Two Sisters in the Spirit: Thérèse of Lisieux and Elizabeth of the Trinity* (San Francisco: Ignatius Press, 1992).

Beausobre, J. de., *Flame in the Snow: St Seraphim of Sarov* (London: Collins, 1979).

Bethge, E., *Dietrich Bonhoeffer: A Biography* (London: Collins, 1970).

Bingaman, B., & Nassif, B., (eds), *The Philokalia: A Classic Text of Orthodox Spirituality* (Oxford: Oxford University Press, 2012).

Boulay, S. de., *Cicely Saunders: The Founder of the Modern Hospice Movement* (London: SPCK, 2007).

Campbell, R. (tr.), *The Poems of St John of the Cross* (London: Harvill Press, 1951).

Chadwick, H., *Augustine of Hippo* (Oxford: Oxford University Press, 2008).

Chadwick, H., *The Early Church* (Harmondsworth: Penguin, 1967).

Chadwick, O., *Michael Ramsey: A Life* (Oxford: Clarendon Press, 1990).

Clare, Mother Mary, *Encountering the Depths* (Oxford: SLG Press, 2014).

Delio, I., *Simply Bonaventure: An Introduction to his Life, Thought & Writings* (New York: New City Press, 2001).

Dumas, A., *Dietrich Bonhoeffer: Theologian of Reality* (London: SCM Press, 1971).

Inge, D. (ed.), *Happiness and Holiness: Thomas Traherne and his Writings* (Norwich: Canterbury Press, 2008).

Isaac, Hieromonk, *Elder Paisios of Mount Athos* (Chalkidiki, Greece: Holy Monastery of St Arsenios, 2012).

James, E. W. (ed.), *Flame in the Mountains: Williams Pantycelyn, Ann Griffiths, and the Welsh Hymn* (Ceredigion: Y Lolfa Cyf, Talybont, 2017).

Jasper, R. C. D., *George Bell: Bishop of Chichester* (Oxford: Oxford University Press, 1967).

Keller, D. G. R. (ed.), *Boundless Grandeur: The Christian Vision of Donald Allchin* (Eugene, OR: Pickwick Publications, 2015).

Knowles, D., *The English Mystical Tradition* (London: Burns & Oates, 1961).

Leclercq, J., *The Love of Learning and the Desire for God* (London: SPCK, 1978).

Palmer, G. E. H., Sherrard P., Ware, Kallistos (tr. & ed.), *The Philokalia*, five vols (London: Faber, 1979–2023).

Peeters, T., *When Silence Speaks: The Spiritual Way of the Carthusian Order* (London: Darton, Longman & Todd, London, 2019).

Porphyrios, *Wounded by Love: The Life & Wisdom of Elder Porphyrios* (Limni, Greece: Denise Harvey, 2003).

Ramsey, A. M., *The Glory of God and the Transfiguration of Christ* (London: Longmans, 1949).

Ramsey, A. M., *From Gore to Temple* (London: Longmans, 1960).

Ramsey, A. M., *Be Still and Know* (London: Collins, 1982).
Ramsey, A. M., *The Gospel & the Catholic Church* (London: SPCK, 1990).
Ramsey, A. M., *The Christian Priest Today* (London: SPCK, 2009).
Ravier, A., *Saint Bruno the Carthusian* (Leominster: Gracewing, 2017).
Sakharov, S., *Saint Silouan the Athonite* (Maldon: Stavropegic Monastery of St John the Baptist, 1991).
Sakharov, S., *We shall see Him as He is* (Maldon: Stavropegic Monastery of St John the Baptist, 2004).
Southern, R. W., *Saint Anselm: A Portrait in a Landscape* (Cambridge: Cambridge University Press, 1990).
Speake, G., *Mount Athos: Renewal in Paradise* (New Haven, CT and London: Yale University Press, 2002).
Stăniloae, D., *The Experience of God* (Brookline, MA: Holy Cross Orthodox Press, 1998).
Vasileios, Archimandrite, *Hymn of Entry* (Crestwood, NY: St Vladimir's Seminary Press, 1998).
Ward, B., *The Prayers & Meditations of St Anselm with the 'Proslogion'* (Harmondsworth: Penguin, 1973).
Ward, B., *The Sayings of the Desert Fathers: The Alphabetical Collection* (London: Mowbray, 1975).
Ward, B., *Harlots of the Desert: A Study of Repentance in Early Monastic Sources* (London: Mowbray, 1987).
Ware, K., *The Orthodox Church* (London: Penguin, 1963).

Ware, K., *The Orthodox Way* (Crestwood, NY: St Vladimir's Seminary Press, 2002).
Williams, R., *On Augustine* (London: Bloomsbury Continuum, 2016).

# Who's Who

**Cicely Saunders**   1918–2005
**Alfonso de Zulueta**   1903–80
**Henry Chadwick**   1920–2008
**Michael Ramsey**   1904–88
**Benedicta Ward**   1933–2022
**Donald Allchin**   1930–2010
**Peter Walker**   1919–2010
**Mary Clare**   1906–88

# Saints

**Aidan** (*d.*651)   missionary and Bishop of Lindisfarne
**Alcuin** (*d.*804)   Abbot of Tours and theologian
**Ann Griffiths** (*d.*1805)   Welsh Christian poet
**Anselm** (*d.*1109)   Archbishop of Canterbury and Doctor of the Church
**Augustine of Canterbury** (*d.*604)   first Archbishop of Canterbury
**Augustine of Hippo** (*d.*430)   bishop and Doctor of the Church
**Bede** (*d.*735)   historian and Doctor of the Church
**Bertha** (*d.*601)   Christian queen of Kent
**Boethius** (*d.*524)   statesman and philosopher
**Bonaventure** (*d.*1274)   Franciscan leader and Doctor of the Church
**Boniface** (*d.*754)   missionary bishop in Germany
**Bruno** (*d.*1101)   founder of the Carthusians
**Cadfan** (*d.*fifth century)   founder of the monastery on Bardsey Island in Wales
**Clare of Assisi**   (*d.*1253)   founder of the Poor Clares
**Columba** (*d.*597)   missionary Abbot of Iona

**David/ Dewi (*d*.601 or 589)**   patron saint of Wales
**Dietrich Bonhoeffer (*d*.1945)**   Lutheran theologian and martyr
**Dunstan (*d*.988)**   Archbishop of Canterbury and monastic reformer
**Elizabeth of the Trinity (*d*.1906)**   Carmelite saint and mystic of Dijon
**Etheldreda (*d*.679)**   Anglo-Saxon Abbess of Ely
**Francis of Assisi (*d*.1226)**   founder of the Franciscans
**Gregory of Sinai (*d*.1346)**   Ascetic theologian of Mount Athos
**Gregory Palamas (*d*.1359)**   ascetic theologian and Archbishop of Thessaloniki
**Gregory the Great (*d*.604)**   pope and Doctor of the Church
**Hilda (*d*.680)**   Anglo-Saxon Abbess of Whitby
**Hugh of Lincoln** *(d.1200)*   Carthusian and Bishop of Lincoln
**John XXIII (*d*.1963)**   pope and saint
**John Climacus**   *(d.649)*   ascetic teacher in Sinai
**John of the Cross (*d*.1591)**   mystical theologian and Doctor of the Church
**John Paul II (*d*.2005)**   pope and saint
**Joseph the Hesychast (*d*.1959)**   hermit on Mount Athos
**Leo the Great (*d*.461)**   pope and Doctor of the Church
**Macarius (*d*.391)**   abbot in the Wadi Natrun in Egypt

**Martin of Tours** (*d*.397)   missionary bishop and monk

**Mary of Egypt** (*d*.sixth century)   hermit in the desert of the Jordan

**Melangell (seventh century)**   Irish hermit in Wales

**Mildred of Thanet** (*d*.700)   Anglo-Saxon Abbess of Minster-in-Thanet

**Newman, John Henry** (*d*.1890)   theologian, cardinal, saint and Doctor of the Church

**Paisios** (*d*.1994)   hermit and spiritual father on Mount Athos

**Patrick** (*d*.461)   missionary bishop in Ireland

**Porphyrios** (*d*.1991)   Athonite hermit and hospital chaplain in Athens

**Romuald** (*d*.1027)   founder of the Camaldolese Benedictines

**Seiriol (sixth century)**   hermit in Anglesey in Wales

**Sergius** (*d*.1392)   Abbot of the Trinity Monastery near Moscow

**Seraphim of Sarov** (*d*.1834)   Russian hermit and spiritual father

**Silouan** (*d*.1938)   Russian monk on Mount Athos

**Sophrony** (*d*.1993)   saint and founder of the Orthodox monastery in Essex

**Symeon the New Theologian** (*d*.1022)   mystic and theologian in Constantinople

**Teresa of Ávila** (*d*.1582)   Carmelite mystic and Doctor of the Church

**Thérèse of Lisieux** (*d*.1897)   Carmelite mystic and Doctor of the Church

**Thomas a Becket (*d*.1170)**   Archbishop of Canterbury and martyr
**Thomas More (*d*.1535)**   statesman and martyr
**Willibrord (*d*.739)**   missionary bishop in the Low Countries

# Other books by Douglas Dales

*Living through Dying: The Spiritual Experience of St Paul*
*Dunstan: Saint and Statesman*
*Light to the Isles: Mission and Theology in*
*Celtic and Anglo-Saxon Britain*
*Alcuin: His Life and Legacy*
*Alcuin: Theology and Thought*
*Divine Remaking: St Bonaventure and the Gospel of Luke*
*Way Back to God: The Spiritual Theology of St Bonaventure*
*Truth & Reality: The Wisdom of St Bonaventure*
*This is my Faith: A Confirmation Book*
*Prayers of our Faith*
*A Mind Intent on God: The Prayers and Spiritual Writings of Alcuin*
*Glory: The Spiritual Theology of Michael Ramsey*
*Glory Descending: Michael Ramsey and His Writings*
*The Spring of Hope: Sermons for the Seasons of Faith*
*The Well of Life: More Sermons for the Seasons of Faith*
*Divine Indwelling: Deification in the Spiritual Theology of St*
*Bonaventure*

EU GPSR Authorized Representative:

LOGOS EUROPE, 9 rue Nicolas Poussin, 17000 La Rochelle, France

contact@logoseurope.eu